"Your Pastor Is an Endangered Species *could not be closer to the nerve of need. Wherever I go, pastors are screaming for help in the areas H.B. London and Neil Wiseman discuss in this book. Never have lay leaders needed such insights as they provide.*"

Howard G. Hendricks
Distinguished Professor, Dallas Theological Seminary
Chairman, Center for Christian Leadership

"*The types of pastors described in chapter 1 have all sought help at Gray Fox Ranch. Thanks to H.B. London and Neil Wiseman for featuring them in their new book and helping the congregations they serve to serve them in return. As a ministry specializing in the care of clergy couples, we always have on hand a large supply of H.B. and Neil's books. This is another one that we will recommend to all.*"

Dr. Walter and Fran Becker
Gray Fox Ranch
Alto, New Mexico

"*H.B. London and Neil Wiseman have provided a way to remove the road-blocks that exist between pastors and their laypeople. Pastors need our love and support. Laypeople need to be encouraged and listened to. We need each other.*"

Gary Smalley
from the Foreword

YOUR PASTOR IS AN ENDANGERED SPECIES

H.B. London, Jr. &
Neil B. Wiseman

VICTOR BOOKS

A DIVISION OF SCRIPTURE PRESS PUBLICATIONS INC.
USA CANADA ENGLAND

Editors: Rachel Derowitsch, Barbara Williams
Design: Scott Rattray
Cover Illustration: Britt Taylor Collins

Library of Congress Cataloging-in-Publication Data

London, H.B.
Your pastor is an endangered species / H.B.
London, Jr. & Neil B. Wiseman.
  p. cm.
  ISBN 1-56476-585-7
1. Clergy—Mental health. 2. Burn out (Psychology)
—Religious aspects—Christianity. 3. Church officers.
I. Wiseman, Neil B. II. Title.
BV4398.L66   1996
253' .2—dc20   96-15082
                                      CIP

CONTENTS

FOREWORD

Today, more than ever before, is a movement of men and women seeking to follow God's will. Husbands and fathers are asking how they can be better equipped to love and lead their families. Wives and mothers are realizing how much influence they have as they give and serve. With this new spirit of growth comes a very dangerous roadblock that could bring this new enthusiasm to a standstill. That roadblock is the strained relationship between pastors and their laypeople.

As a former pastor, I have tremendous empathy for all the pressures that pastors face as they try to meet the needs of their congregations. I always knew when somebody in my church was not happy with me or my performance. The expectations of meeting so many different needs were overwhelming. I went home many nights feeling as if I just could not do enough to measure up to everyone's expectations. I saw many of the laypeople as a threat instead of as a partner.

Many churches today are going through difficult times even in the middle of a new spirit of growth and commitment. I believe that H.B. London and Neil Wiseman have provided a way to remove the roadblocks that exist between pastors and laypeople. Pastors need our love and support. Laypeople need to be encouraged and listened to. We need each other.

The differences between pastors and laypeople can be solved. Pastors and laypeople need to begin to share a joint vision, to put their differences behind them, and move forward in obedience to the call of God. We need to listen to each other's dreams and needs. We need to learn how to resolve our conflicts and listen to God's plan for our lives. Pastors need affirmation and appreciation. They often live in fear that no one really cares or listens. Laypeople need a strategy that gives them opportunities to use their gifts and talents.

This book is a call to genuine spiritual renewal throughout the whole church. If we cannot or will not pay the price for this renewal, the consequences to the church around the world will be tragic.

Gary Smalley
President of Today's Family

PREFACE

Some have questioned our choice of title—*Your Pastor Is an Endangered Species*—but from our vantage point it is obvious that the church and those who lead her are in a struggle for meaningful exsistence. They are threatened and endangered.

What Do Threatened and Endangered Mean?

Threatened means that a species or segment of a vocation or population sampling may become endangered in the near future. In the animal and plant families a species is called "threatened" when numbers have gotten so low that it soon may be hard to produce enough replacements to keep the species healthy. What is healthy? Numbers large enough to survive normal threats to its continuance.

Endangered means that a species may become extinct. A species is endangered when numbers are so low or weakened that unless we "do something" there will soon be no more of that species left in the world.

We may scoff at this, but when you apply these definitions to the animal and plant families, the list totals almost 1,000 either endangered or threatened species in the U.S.

Endangered pastors and full-time Christian workers exceed 1 million. It seems, like threatened and endangered species, our North American pastors struggle for recognition as spiritual leaders. Forced terminations are at record numbers. Our figures point out that at least 25 percent of all active pastors have experienced the pain of a difficult severance. Further, when clergy reach the age of two score and ten, they become less desirable to a congregation than their younger, less experienced colleagues. More than 90 percent of all clergy couples feel the pressure to be an ideal role model, yet their families are in many cases dysfunctional and unhappy. Salaries are inadequate, retirement benefits insufficient, and in most cases clergy are lonely with few friends, thus receiving very little affirmation and encouragement.

The latest figures by the Barna Research Group reveal other troubling statistics. More than four out of five Americans call themselves Christian, but less than half (37 percent) attend church services in a given week. This makes the shepherd's job even more difficult because the sheep are so scattered. It is estimated that 40 percent of those presently serving the church body will not be doing so ten years from now.

In spite of these startling and seemingly depressing statistics, we feel hopeful. There is a way to reverse the tide of endangerment and return the church and those called to lead it to their rightful place of honor, respect, and prominence within our society.

What can we do? Perhaps we can learn a few things from the world of nature where biologists and landowners are finding ways to help keep species from dying out. Some plans they use to preserve the future of animals and plants include setting aside special areas for wildlife habitat; decreasing or changing the use of certain pesticides and herbicides; managing livestock or crops; and preserving wildlife areas. One of the most important things these people do is share information with one another so they make rational life-saving decisions about endangered or threatened species.

Can we do any less for our spiritual leaders? The future of our beloved church and those who have been called to guide her are at stake. In these next "prayed-over" pages we will attempt to enlighten you, encourage you, challenge you, and even at some points correct you. What we say here we say in love and genuine concern for the church who has opened her arms to us and for our colleagues who have grown to depend on us. We believe there is hope for your pastor who in so many cases has become an endangered species.

And now, friends, we ask you to honor those leaders who work so hard for you, who have been given the responsibility of urging and guiding you along in your obedience. Overwhelm them with appreciation and love (1 Thes. 5:12-13).

— H.B. and Neil

"Jesus cleansed the meaning of greatness when He said, 'The greatest among you shall be the servant of all.' No longer is the man great who has a great number of servants, but that man is great who serves the greatest number."

E. Stanley Jones

1. PASTORS UNDER FIRE
Can't Something Be Done Now ?

God, the Great Head of the church,
> *I rejoice in the privilege of serving You in Your church.*
> *Help our congregation, especially me, to cherish our pastor more.*
> *We are grateful for our pastor's ministry.*
> *Thanks for calling our minister into Your service.*
> *Thanks too for calling our pastor to this place.*
> *Enable us to serve together—pastor and people—as if this were our*
> > *last day, or better still as if it were our first. Amen.*

Serving as a pastor seems like Marcie's experience in a *Peanuts* cartoon. Marcie felt incredible frustration when she tried to kick a football; it fell on her head rather than floating downfield. She observed dejectedly, "When I kicked the ball, my glasses, my sock, and my shoe all flew off, and the ball came down and hit me on the head!" Then she added an aside to Charlie Brown, "Football is a humorous game, isn't it, sir?"

Charlie Brown replied philosophically, "Humorous if you aren't serious about football." Ministry is like that too. High demands matched against slow results might be humorous if your pastor were not serious about representing Christ in our time—the only time we have.

Today's pastors face crises unknown to any other occupational groups. Contemporary parish ministry, without anyone intending to make it so, has become an emotional and spiritual H-bomb, ready to

15

explode any second. Demands are up. Credibility is down. Suspicions are up. And needs are up. Comrades are going AWOL at the front lines, choosing to become therapists, gas station attendants, or carpenters instead of pastors. Meanwhile, ministry preparation programs and theological education institutions seem out of touch with reality in parish, community, and world realities. Increasing hordes of dysfunctional people in the general population mean more emotionally crippled, spiritually handicapped, and relationally wounded people are in every church. Time and financial commitments keep getting more and more complicated for clergy couples and lay families. Volunteer lay leaders have less time to devote to the church. Rising living standards steal time from marriage and parenting obligations. And specialization in many other occupational fields makes people expect more from a pastor's preaching, teaching, counseling, leadership, and financial competencies.

Look Over H.B.'s Shoulder at the Mail

Hundreds of letters addressed to Focus on the Family describe excruciatingly painful situations many pastors face in contemporary ministry settings. Some problems are deeply rooted in the culture. Church pillars, to make improvements in society, must intentionally create a counterculture that keeps a congregation different from the environment where it does its ministry for Christ. Unless a church is different from secular society, the church and society are both on the ropes. Many difficulties in the church call for decisive renewal, deepened commitment, and spiritual passion. The church must give more attention to protecting and encouraging pastors. Its future is in jeopardy if it continues killing her wounded frontline soldiers.

Here's a sample letter from a pastor similar to many others:

Dear H.B.: We'll be leaving the pastoral ministry once and for all in a few days. My family, especially my wife, cannot continue to survive the continuous stress of a church. I must leave pastoral ministry to remain faithful to God—maybe to save my soul. I have felt so constrained by the politics of the whole thing that I have not been a spiritual leader. I am a title holder. I do pastoral things. If I were to describe my church and denomination, I would say "spiritually dead, yet physically functioning." Pulling the right strings without making waves has been a killer. I can say that if someone were not praying for us, I would walk away to call myself an atheist. In spite of people and problems, the Lord Jesus Christ has preserved my faith. . . . Since speaking with my denomination leaders and fellow pastors, I find that five out of eight of us have been or are living under the same oppression we're leaving. My heart goes out to them. It amazes me that they, too, do not go on to other ministries or secular work. I have great compassion for them, for they are in need.

Pay attention to the spirit of the letter to hear those phrases that describe this pastor's pain and broken dreams:
  • I can't survive the continued stress.
  • I must leave to be faithful to God.
  • I have not been a spiritual leader but a title holder.
  • My church is spiritually dead but physically functioning.
  • Pulling the right strings has been a killer.
  • Without prayers, I would have walked away an atheist.

Is it possible that your pastor faces comparable concerns? If yes, why not do something to improve the situation?

For the contemporary church, the mandate is for lay leaders to help pastors by coming alongside them and their families to facilitate spiritual restoration and renewal. Pastors need help to better manage their time, finances, and lives. Like Moses, they need someone to hold up their hands in battle and to perform lesser duties so they can give themselves to eternal kingdom concerns. Ministers need someone to free them from minutia so they can do what God called them to do. Ministers need someone to befriend them, to care for them, and to lovingly keep them accountable for essentials.

Let's consider the implications of current difficulty: when pastors are at risk, the church of Jesus Christ is also at risk. As we talk with pastors, spend long hours after conferences, ride to and from airports, and read the mail, we hear a cry from their hearts. They want to do ministry, to help transform lives, to make a significant difference, but they feel stymied by pressures, constraints, and frustrations.

Sometimes we want to take pastors' hands to assure them everything will be okay. But we are not convinced it will be okay until the church of Jesus Christ sees the problems and local congregations do something to fix them. We are not sure it will be okay until all believers see we are in this struggle together—pastors and pillars and congregations. That's a powerful team that can do great things for God. But if we are to make even a small dent in winning the world, we have to have spiritually strong pastors. We need fulfilled pastors who love doing the work of ministry. We need pastors who really believe committed laity will help them. We must have pastors who are provided the best possible opportunities to do ministry, including education, spiritual foundations, affirmation, encouragement, facilities, salary, and tools.

Collision of Expectations

Listen to the collision of confusing expectations from an ad written by a pulpit committee in a western state, recently published in a pastors' magazine:

> Seeking an exceptional, committed individual for unique ministry in central [name of state] willing to help us survive and reach our potential and be an active participant in maintaining a strong Christian witness with a stable congregation of 40 members, all ages. A National Park is close, golf and fishing are convenient. Other recreational opportunities are within easy driving distance. Rock hounding paradise. This is a challenge. Prospective pastors must be willing to experience new perspectives, different culture, and great satisfaction. Tent-making or part-time position. [1]

Think of the unrealistic demands in that ad: Come be a tent-maker pastor so you can serve forty church members. They want a pastor who can help them survive, fulfill their potential, and maintain a strong witness. All of these expectations are to be accomplished by a person who welcomes new perspectives and a different culture. After reading the ad, one wag remarked, "Too bad they can't find someone who walks on water, flies without wings, and hunts antelope for food."

Contrast that ad with what ministers consider to be their most important priorities. A recent study showed pastors think a fulfilling marriage, followed by the challenge of preaching, a sense of calling to the ministry, and satisfaction from pastoral care to be the most significant ministry enhancers. Yet these concerns apparently have low priority or perhaps no importance for the pastoral search committee who placed the ad seeking a pastor for a church of forty persons. No wonder the church is experiencing confusion in so many places.

Such diametrically opposing viewpoints tend to create volatile and fragile relationships between a minister and a congregation. To build bridges between the perspective of pastors who feel under fire and the viewpoint of congregations who feel confused, let's meet several pastors, whose names have been changed, now serving at the front lines of ministry. They are examples of pastors who need parishioners to understand and to help renew the sagging spirit of so many churches.

By getting acquainted with these servants of the church, you can observe firsthand how ministry has become more complex than it has ever been. However, in spite of all the confusing changes, pastors must be given resources to revitalize their ministry, given opportunities for personal renewal, and encouraged to build a strong marriage. Congregations must help pastors design strategies to effectively meet personal challenges and at the same time respond with new energy and imagination to the ever-changing demands the church faces. The spiritual strength of a pastor's ministry is often shaped by how these issues are viewed by lay leaders. A pastor's Christlike character is among a church's most precious possessions—it must be cherished and encouraged at all costs.

Jack Brownstone: Walk-on-water Syndrome Pastor
Ministerial training programs taught Jack that Christ and the church deserve competency. Then as he graduated and took his first church, he tried to apply a standard of excellence to all he did. He worked hard every day to become a gifted speaker, effective administrator,

skilled fund-raiser, competent counselor, sensitive listener, and faithful pastor.

But will, do everything for everyone

He experienced another common internal conflict. Pastors who conscientiously try to do ministry effectively sometimes have difficulty delegating assignments to others. They fear the work will not get done, or they worry that they may get mediocre results.

Meanwhile, church members expected Jack to walk on water, preach like Jesus and pray like Paul. They expected him to have ESP, be at more than one place at the same time, and have a fulfilling marriage and flawless children. Some church members felt annoyed when they discovered no human being, not even one especially called of God, could live up to what they expected.

These issues are the main reason nearly two-thirds of pastors feel immobilized by congregational expectations. [2]

This walk-on-water syndrome sometimes hurts ministers in another way by encouraging them to believe their own press reports. Affirmed by their members as being superpastors, they begin to believe all the nice things parishioners say about them and believe they can do no wrong, no one else can do everything as well as they can, and they deserve every privilege they can orchestrate. In the process, it is easy to become obnoxiously ego-centered.

The Apostle Peter taught us in the Bible about walking on water. He demonstrated how walking on water was impossible for human beings. He also learned quickly that one can drown when he takes his eyes off of Christ.

Church pillars shouldn't expect pastors to be experts at everything. They're not. To find happy relationships, pastor and people should cultivate an accurate awareness of what needs to be done in ministry in contemporary culture. They must discover what the pastor and lay leader can do at this time, in this place. And no pastor should be expected to do any task a lay person can do effectively.

Here's another way of viewing high expectations, with our apology to Bill Vaughan for paraphrasing his essay "Dad Asks for Tolerance on First Day of School":

I thought today as he (the pastor) strode bravely off to church.

20

His sensitivity, his gentleness, his inquiring mind, his very physical well-being are for you to nurture or to wound.... Would you be a little extra nice to him? Give him a smile? When he makes a mistake, as he will, try to ignore it or at least give him another chance? He's really quite dedicated you know.... He believes in church and holy living, and even if it doesn't mean as much to you as it does to him, will you let him down easy? And remember this: it may make no difference to you he's your pastor, but he is also my son. So take it easy, huh?

Tom Adams: A Moral Crusading Pastor

Troubled by decaying conditions in our contemporary culture, Tom Adams can be counted on to preach about vanishing absolutes. He often thunders prophetic utterances from his pulpit about murder, lying, stealing, adultery, and the worship of the modern idols of secularism. Recently he preached against adultery, including the emotional kind. And he preached against stealing, even tax evasion, and about how habitual gossipers steal good reputations. He was biblical, prophetic, and quite specific.

What an uproar followed—a kind of emotional earthquake. Many people were steaming mad but did not want Tom to know how much his preaching bothered them. But Tom recognized their displaced anger—outrage over a minor issue that stems from some apparently unrelated issue.

Now, however, he feels confused. Should he deal with what he thinks are "real issues," or try to put out tiny fires like a shrill scolding he received from a church member for the way he conducted Communion last Sunday? In his bewilderment, Tom goes to an influential laywoman to ask for advice; she advises him to stop all controversy in his preaching. After the conversation, he gets even more confused over his duty to declare demanding truths from Scripture and the need to keep complainers happy. He can't see how he can do both.

It's a tough call. At a time when 67 percent of Americans say there is no such thing as absolute truth, it is difficult to preach about moral absolutes and keeping the Ten Commandments; in many places they are now regarded as the "ten suggestions." What was once considered absolute truth is now considered mere opinion. Americans have moved from measuring our lives by Scripture to doing what is right in our own eyes. The contemporary crisis is proof that "there is a way that seems right to a man, but in the end it leads to death" (Prov. 14:12). Regrettably, this attitude has seeped into churches as well, so everyone does what is right in his own sight without regard to what God wants. Meanwhile, society dies a slow, miserable suicide because we have given up on the virtues of self-control, compassion, tolerance, faith, integrity, morality, and respect for authority. No civilization can survive such a loss.

Greg Brooks: New Breed Bi-vocational Pastor

Greg Brooks, age thirty, and his wife, Carol, serve a fifty-year-old, seventy-member church in a town of 8,000 in the heartland. They have two children, ages four and six.

For years this church had been pastored by ministers who were willing to live below the poverty line while church members enjoyed a middle-class lifestyle. Such sacrifices by the minister's family were expected; no one questioned the arrangement. Whenever personal economic disasters happened to former pastors, they took part-time jobs in a grocery store owned by a church member.

Things are different since Greg arrived, though the church's financial compensation hasn't changed much. Greg has a computer drafting skill, so he sends his freelance work by modem to his employer's office in a distant city. He usually works about twenty hours per week in his home at his drafting duties, which produce more income than the church pays him. As a result, he lives at a comfortable middle-class lifestyle, drives the kind of car he wants, and clothes his family at the same level as his parishioners.

Recently, the church offered Greg a $3,000 annual raise provided he work full-time for the church. That would make his cash salary from the church $10,000 per year, plus housing and utilities. When Greg declined, several old-time church members questioned his commitment to ministry—without considering his and his wife's educational loans, which amounted to more than $25,000 when they graduated from seminary. Neither did the questioners think about the future college funds needed for the children. Nor did they think to compare their standard of living with his.

It has become a touchy, hush-hush situation, so no one in the official decision group discusses it with Greg. Nonetheless, a continuous murmuring can be heard throughout the congregation. Deep down, even the critics know they would rather have Greg as pastor on a bi-vocational basis than others who aren't willing to scrimp along on small wages.

No one knows where this confusion between Greg and this church will lead. But just below the surface, there are several issues that all church pillars need to consider about their pastor's salary:

• Can a pastor maintain a middle-class standard of living on the current compensation package? Does your church want its pastor to live at the poverty line?

• Can a pastor repay from his current pay level his educational expenses incurred in ministry training?

• How much latitude should a low-paying church allow its pastor when he is doing his ministry as well or better than a person of more limited ability who serves full-time? As one wise, old leader in a small church said, "I'd rather have our present pastor part–time than most pastors full-time."

• Why not discuss economic issues in a non-judgmental way with your pastor so you see the issues from his perspective? How do the financial issues look to him?

• Can you expect a pastor to live at the lowest economic level of any member of the church? Often the most outspoken negative voice in a decision group is someone who makes less than the pastor, and that person's cloudy perspective is not realistic about the pastor's actual financial needs.

Unlike many other professionals, pastors are limited in ways to earn extra income. Thus, they often feel locked in by their present economic situation. Because their pay package has been low for so many years, most ministers need more than a token annual increase or a cost-of-living raise. Long years of low income keep many ministers under constant financial pressures. Someone needs to champion significant raises in every church where it can be done. Being locked into financial prisons makes pastors weary, causes them to lose the challenge for their work, and tempts them to quit so they can become better providers for their families.

Craig Eades: The Emotionally Exhausted Pastor
Craig serves a growing suburban congregation of mostly new believers who, for the most part, have been employed in factories of the Great Lakes region for years. Some of the families have been employed by the same company for several generations. Now the information age has dawned and many factories have closed, displacing many workers. Some have lost jobs; others have taken lesser-paying jobs; while others wonder if they will be the next to be unemployed.

Many new converts were first attracted to Craig's church because it offered peace, wholeness, and stability. Some have dysfunctional pasts, including abuse, broken marriages, eroded self-esteem, and drug and alcohol addictions. Old-timers in the church have no frame of reference for understanding the magnitude of these problems or the massive increase these needs create in a pastor's workload. Though it is seldom mentioned, effective evangelism simply increases demands—the more people find Christ, the more churches will serve people who bring incredible entanglements with them.

In addition to the problems of his church members, Craig carries scars from his own emotionally fractured childhood. His wife, Mary, has hurts from when her father deserted their family when she was six. Trying to be a Christian family takes hard work for Craig and Mary. They consider such a struggle important to their personal wholeness, and they believe a good marriage serves as a model of what a strong Christian home should be. Though Craig and Mary are deeply committed to each other and to their children, they are forced to deal with their own emotional impairments even as they work to help heal the wounds of people in the congregation.

Recently, Mary told a mentoring friend she and Craig felt "emotionally spent" because they faced so many problems in church members' lives. She also confessed that she felt terrorized by emotional and relationship crises they observed in pastoral peers. Mary sees no relief in sight because these crises of problem people inside and outside the church will not likely lessen. Instead, they may increase. Pastors are caught in the middle between dysfunction and healing.

Pillars in the church may have trouble understanding this heavy load for a pastor. Because laypersons don't face these problems very often or for long, they should not be expected to comprehend how much emotional and spiritual energy these problems drain from a pastor. Since these components of ministry are so confidential, a pastor can't talk with anyone about them. He is forced to bear this burden alone. Taking the strength of the Lord into dysfunctional lives is rewarding but fatiguing work.

What can church pillars do to help pastors carry these heavy duties? They can offer several supports to their pastor.

• Understand your pastor. When he seems preoccupied or pensive, try to understand that he may be dealing with confusing issues concerning someone's hurts. The greatest demands are often issues that are the most confidential.

• Encourage your pastor to take a break. Help her take a break from her duties by inviting her to lunch or coffee without discussing church work. Invite your pastor to a social or athletic event that will help her set aside the needs of hurting people for a few hours.

• Help troubled people in your church. Become a listener or leaning post to someone who has problems you understand or have experienced. Often a simple statement of affirmation such as, "I'm glad to see you growing in Christ," encourages an individual to get his focus off the problem and on Christ. When you do this, you give an overworked pastor some needed relief.

• Offer to become a spiritual mentor to new converts. Teach them how to pray. Show them how to read the Bible. Encourage them in every possible way. Keep close enough so they are willing to share the frustrations of their pilgrimage with you. Like raising an infant, caring for a new convert is often frustrating. In spite of the demands, however, it often pays off in the long run and keeps the new convert from demanding too much emotional support from the pastor. Everyone wins in such an effort: you help the new convert, you relieve the pastor, and in the process you enjoy the satisfaction such ministry produces.

Your Pastor Is an Endangered Species

Rick Shields: The AWOL Pastor

Rick Shields fits the traditional image of a good pastor. Faithful, loyal, trustworthy, steady, he apparently loves everybody and is loved in return.

But one day he mysteriously disappeared, leaving his wife and nearly grown children and deserting his church—an AWOL pastor. Friends and family couldn't think of any logical reasons for his disappearance: perhaps he might have experienced a blackout, or had an affair, or was trying to run away from some dark secret. Because he was so faithful, some feared Rick was a victim of foul play. No one could believe he would walk off without telling anyone.

After a few days, his wife filed a missing person's report. An all-points police bulletin was issued across several states. No one came up with a clue. Rick didn't use his checking account or credit cards. No one heard from him for nearly six months. Finally, Rick called his wife, telling her to get a divorce and spend their combined assets. He said he wanted a new life in a new place with a new identity. He took a new name and applied for a new Social Security card. He wanted a job dealing with things rather than people.

Rick's story is dramatic and probably won't happen to any pastor you know. But many pastors have left a thousand times in their minds. Many others stay but have quietly stopped being daring or productive.

How does it happen? Trivia becomes too heavy. Apathy among lay leaders suffocates. Rick did nearly everything in his church, and the people let him. He cut grass, painted buildings, preached sermons, deposited offerings, visited the sick, raised his kids under the critical scrutiny of church members, and did nearly everything his wife wanted him to do.

Rick played by the rules, staying in the game for twenty years. In phone interviews since leaving, he said, "I couldn't cope with secular values in the church and felt responsible to correct moral chaos outside the church. I left because I could not make a difference, so why keep trying. I became weary of those who think a minister doesn't work when he is bi-vocational. I paid most of the bills at my churches for years. I thought my sacrifice was wasted, so I saw no point in continuing."

Consider Rick's perspective—he didn't quit because he gave up on God but because he thought the cause was no longer worthy of his investment. What if he were right?

Church pillars must realize that some pastors would quit immediately if they had another way to support themselves. Lay leaders can prevent much of this pain of a destroyed dream by giving attention to the care and feeding of their pastor. Ask yourself what you can do to help your pastor find fulfillment in his work. Help him keep the church rooted in authentic spiritual issues. Seldom do pastors burn out or quit during spiritual breakthroughs; it happens during shallow, tough times when the work is frustrating and the results slow.

Ask yourself and others often if your church is doing the main business of Christ in your setting for the right reasons. Does your congregation deserve a God-called person to give years of his life to its ministry? Or is your church a kingdom outpost that expects pastors to keep the store, maintain routines, and keep everyone happy—including the spiritually immature and fringe folks? Is your fellowship a place where a pastor will look back in twenty years and think every sacrifice was worth it? Is it a church where he will remember spiritual breakthroughs you experienced together and be able to recall those who were rescued from the despair of their sinful lives?

Wayne Carlson: The Marriage and Ministry Competition Pastor
College sweethearts, Wayne and Jan married on the day they graduated from college. As they moved on to seminary life, Jan immediately started feeling Wayne's studies and their marriage were in competition. Wayne felt pulled between his studies, in which he wanted to do well, and his marriage, in which he wanted to be the best husband any woman ever had. Competition between marriage and ministry continued into the pastorate.

Wayne allowed himself to become a ministry workaholic who fooled himself into believing he was doing something magnificent for God even though he was compulsively overcommitted. Wayne and Jan grew apart more and more. However, she continued to work two days per week as a nurse at the nearby hospital, giving the rest of her energies to being a homemaker and good mother to their two children. Their emotional and physical distance was obvious to everyone around them, but outsiders thought it was the normal chemistry of their relationship. Both were alarmingly vulnerable to outside emotional attachments, and Wayne kept himself too busy to heed the witherings in his own heart.

Soon Wayne became sexually involved with a female counselee. He never intended that an innocent flirtation would take him that far. But his moral temptations started with a thousand smaller issues that went wrong in his ministry and marriage. He simply couldn't see his need for balance. At any rate, ministry is apparently over for Wayne and Jan.

Of course, infidelity is sinfully wrong. It annihilates pastoral credibility and integrity. It sabotages everything a pastor has accomplished for God. It violates people, breaks up marriages, and crushes children. And lay leaders, after such a failure, are nearly always helpless to restore the pastor.

Can lay leaders do something to prevent a pastor's infidelity? Every church can encourage its pastor to view a healthy marriage as of great importance to being a whole person. Every church needs a whole pastor preaching from its pulpit. And every church needs a beautiful model of Christian marriage and family life lived out in front of its people. Thus, every effort at prevention is important.

Church pillars do their pastors and congregations an important favor by encouraging their pastor to find balance between marriage and ministry. A great marriage is a fine gift a pastor gives himself, but it is also an important ministry given to the church. As a lay leader in the church, encourage your pastor to cultivate a strong, stable, happy marriage. Push him to take the time and effort to do that. Suggest he take time away with his wife. If needed, raise money outside regular giving channels so your ministry couple can get away together; it will pay rather than cost. Apply creativity and imagination to help your pastor and spouse find a retreat center within driving distance; perhaps somebody in the church has a cabin or summer home or motor home. Someone might help purchase plane tickets for your ministry couple to take a trip.

Prevention also might include Christian counseling. If your pastor needs counseling, help foot the bill as a favor to your church as well as to your pastor.

Though no one can take responsibility for the strength of another person's marriage, church pillars can help with affirmation, influence, and encouragement. Remember three important facts: (1) pastors are alarmingly vulnerable to outside emotional temptations during times of disheartening hopelessness; (2) a good marriage is an important energizer for effective ministry—every effort to strengthen a clergy marriage is an empowerment to a pastor's ministry; and (3) a church seldom, if ever, completely recovers from a pastor's infidelity.

God never intended ministry and marriage to be in competition. When such competition exists, someone must change it.

Toby Moore: The Fearful/Victimized Pastor

The consumer mentality seeping into the church is driving some pastors crazy with fear. It is estimated that as many as 80 percent of all church membership gains in a recent year were a result of people leaving one church and joining another. Like choosing a hairdresser, cleaners, supermarket, or mechanic, people choose churches because of the facilities, programs, and personality of the preacher rather than on the basis of beliefs and doctrine.

Sometimes believers move to another church without explanation and with almost no reason. Sometimes they find a better church nursery or more convenient parking near the church's front door. Sometimes they hear about a big-name concert, so they leave to attend the concert, never to return.

Membership migration frightens ministers. About the time they get ministries going, someone else leaves. Before long, they reason, why try when someone else may leave next Sunday? Every loss fuels feelings of despair for the pastor who cherishes relationships. Soon he starts believing the church is always going to be the way it is now.

Church pillars can discourage member migration by conscientiously listening to concerns and doing something about them. Too often a pastor suggests improvements that are rejected by the decision group; these refusals are often the reason people leave. Stand alongside your pastor in these matters. Encourage people to believe they never need to go anywhere else because this church loves them and wants to serve them in every possible way. When membership losses come, as they will, try telling your pastor that you can win others to take their places. Create a church climate where nobody wants to leave. Implement the reality that every church already has more people near its doors than it can ever hope to reach. Perhaps the time has arrived to work harder at winning new people and assimilating them into the fellowship of the church than worrying about the migration of members.

Mike Wiley: An Invisible Casualties Pastor

Handsome, outgoing, and well-dressed, Mike Wiley told me his story while I shopped for a sport coat at a Kansas City men's store. When in our conversation he discovered I was a friendly advocate for pastors, he told me his unbelievable experience. After scratching economically to finish seminary, Mike and his wife took their first charge among loving people in a small church who knew effective pastors did not stay long. This church had lots of experience affirming pastors, only to see them move to a larger assignment in a year or two. Mike and his wife, just as the church leaders expected, followed the familiar pattern.

At the second church and after having two children in six years, Mike's wife reached a breaking point. She said, "I am tired of the petty gossip about our family, so I'm leaving. You keep the kids. I want freedom."

Mike stayed on at the church for nearly a year, trying to be a single father and pastor. The going was rough—he had to be mom and dad, clean the house, cook the meals, do laundry, and try to be a good pastor. Finally, in absolute exhaustion, he left the church because he couldn't keep "all the balls in the air." Even though the congregation tried to understand him and help with the children, he felt he had to leave. When Mike suggested leaving, church leaders agreed it would not work for him to continue. Now he is among the church's invisible casualties, one of the walking wounded. He's one of the emotionally, spiritually afflicted and forgotten.

Most Sundays, Mike takes the children to a neighborhood church of a denomination different than the one he served. He sells men's clothing during the week to earn a living. He doubts whether he will ever return to the ministry. Even though he tries to put his former church members in the best possible light, he sometimes feels twinges of bitterness. I told him I understood his pain and reminded him that bitterness always poisons those who hold it.

But someone is responsible for his plight. Do gossipers in his former church bear responsibility? Or does the fault belong to his wife? Or perhaps Mike lost his wife because he took his work too seriously. Or does someone else bear blame for stifling his idealism, for perpetuating his poverty, or invading his privacy? Perhaps all parties bear some blame.

Mike is one of the unobtrusive casualties most people don't think about when discussing the pastoral crises in our time. What will Mike feel in fifteen years when he recalls his dreams of Christian service when he started? What will his children remember, and what did they miss? And what about the loss to churches that could have received so much from Mike's ministry?

It's sad to hear a person say, "I used to be a pastor but it just didn't work out." What he means is, "My dream died and someone killed it." Can the church continue to allow her wounded to die without heroic efforts to save them?

What You Might Like to Know about a Pastor's World

Now you have met flesh-and-blood, real-life pastors whose problems are pressing and common. Don't you agree pastors are an interesting and highly committed group? Don't you also agree there is lots of pain among pastors and their families, some of which can be easily remedied by church pillars?

Let's be sure we have a clear picture of the typical pastor's world today in North America. Pastors live in a world that never stops, where the light never goes out, and where the average work week is between fifty-five and seventy-five hours. One in eight are bi-vocational or multi-vocational, and 70 percent of their spouses work outside the home—meaning either or both are secularly employed to keep themselves in ministry.

Pastors dwell in a world of the unfinished tyranny, where they

can't shut the door, walk out of the office, or know something is completely finished. There's always another Bible study, sermon, phone call, committee, hospital call, home visit, or gathering clamoring for attention. When someone dies or gets married or is hospitalized, the well-crafted schedule has to be abandoned and caught up later. Sometimes "later" is a long time coming.

Pastors live in a world of guilt about their families. Most want a Christ-exalting family life that models marriage and parenting for their congregation. But that's tough to accomplish when they often spend more time with other people's kids than they spend with their own and more time with other adults than with their spouse.

Pastors reside in a world of decreasing approval. Where a pastor was once among the most visible, well-educated and revered citizens, a recent Gallup Poll shows clergy are ranked fifty-sixth out of one hundred admired professionals. The Bakkers, Swaggarts, and many lesser-known ministers have forgotten that when they fall morally or compromise their integrity, they not only destroy their credibility and hurt innocent people, they also negatively impact every brother or sister in ministry.

Pastors serve in a me-centered world where church members and attenders are becoming more and more apathetic. As you remember, Jesus promised to build His church so that the gates of hell would never prevail against it (Matt. 16:18). Perhaps the passage might be paraphrased to say the "saints of the church cannot prevail against it." In a day of decaying morality, it is becoming more and more difficult to speak the truth, even in church. So we grasp for new ways, new paradigms, new methods, and forget the old mission and the everlasting message. In many corners of the church, we have watered down the message of the Gospel until it's hardly recognizable. Some pastors doubt whether they can make much of a difference in times like these. Consequently, pastors who want their lives to count are asking if ministry is worth the effort when compared with the results.

Our situation is bleak, but we can change it. The present problem reminds me of a recent TV interview. A supervising physician, head of the trauma center at Parkland Hospital in Dallas, was asked about the revoked federally mandated speed limits on freeways. He replied with

32

anguish, "When speed limits are increased, our trauma cases will increase by at least twenty percent. I don't know who will care for those hurting, sick, dying people if we cannot find more doctors, more nurses, more budget. We're at capacity now most of the time—we just do not have a margin for all the increase."

The doctor's comments sound similar to the current situation in many churches. Just at a time when the world needs pastors more than ever, some drastic steps must be taken to encourage, renew, restore, resource, compensate, and love pastors into greatness. We are losing ground in the clergy personnel pool with fewer recruits, forced resignations, increased early retirements, and more pastors who are running in place and not getting anywhere.

Ultimately, the issue is spiritual, not vocational or cultural. The church has become passionless in many ways. We are lukewarm. The church sits powerless, like a shell without powder, looking the part but not making much difference. And as we sit and talk and pray and cry with pastors, they ask, "What do we have to do? What do we have to say? Where do we have to go? What lengths do we have to take?"

Can't something be done now?

RENEWAL STRATEGIES FOR CHURCH PILLARS
How to Lower the Risks Your Pastor Faces

1. Create a counterculture so your church is always different from the world.

2. Cherish your minister's Christlike character as a priceless asset for your church.

3. Realize when pastors are under fire the church is at serious risk.

4. Come alongside your pastor to facilitate renewal and restoration.

5. Do your part to keep your pastor from becoming a victim of ministry stress.

6. Champion the cause of making congregational expectations reasonable.

7. Question or even confront your pastor about his work schedule.

8. Understand when your pastor is pensive. She may be dealing with an overwhelming problem in someone's life.

9. Keep asking the decision group if your church is doing the main business of Christ in your setting for the right reasons.

10. Try viewing issues from the perspective of Jesus.

"*The attitude Christ modeled for us is one that should typify every Christian, whether in pulpit or pew, whether leader of a vast organization or solitary prayer warrior. Not puffed up with self-importance, but poured out for others.*"

Charles Colson

2. WHAT THE PLAYBOOK SAYS
Biblical Instructions for Church Pillars

Giver and Preserver of Holy Scripture,
I praise You for the written Word,
for its guidance for lay leaders,
for its instruction to pastors,
for its direction for our church.
Help us lay leaders to see Your church as a holy force for
righteousness in our world.
Help me see our church's potentiality as You see it. Amen.

No matter how talented or informed you may be concerning lay leadership, it's essential to occasionally review your understanding of how God uses human beings to accomplish His work through His church. The Bible offers insights concerning lay ministry on nearly every page. It supplies guidance for healthy relationships between leaders and followers and between pastors and parishioners. It's time to read the playbook again and to do what it says.

Scriptural counsel helps us reenergize disheartened pastors. The Bible offers God's wisdom, correction, and perspective to help us shake off lethargy rooted in the secular environment. In the process, every congregation is enriched by clergy and lay leaders who live close to the Bible. It's a win-win situation for everyone.

Consider several biblical passages that provide a clear direction on becoming an effective lay leader.

God Wants Strong Pastors for Developing Leaders

"It was He [Christ] who gave some to be apostles, some to be prophets, some to be evangelists, and some to be pastors and teachers, to prepare God's people for works of service, so that the body of Christ may be built up, until we all reach unity in the faith and in the knowledge of the Son of God, and become mature, attaining to the whole measure of the fullness of Christ" (Eph. 4:11-13).

In a world where confidence for ministers seems at an all-time low, pastors are needed more than ever. We know the community needs religious leaders. We know Christianity needs public spokespersons. We know the church needs pastors, but why?

The church needs pastors to help everyone become Christlike. In many places these days, Ephesians 4:11-13 has become a favorite preaching passage to make the point that one of a pastor's main assignments is "to prepare God's people for works of service." But there is so much more in the verse and the context.

Why does the church need pastors, and why do you need a pastor? In this passage, the Apostle Paul lists nine significant reasons:

1. To build up the body of Christ.
2. To assist us in achieving unity in the faith.
3. To expand our knowledge of the Son of God.
4. To facilitate our maturity.
5. To aid us in attaining the whole measure of the fullness of Christ.
6. To encourage our growth so we will not be deceived by counterfeit teachings.
7. To call us to speak the truth in love.
8. To help us grow up in Christ.
9. To stimulate Christian love so the church will be built up as each part does its work.

As you review Paul's reasons why pastors are needed, it appears these concerns are seldom addressed by anyone except faithful pastors. That's an important reason why pastors are needed, so believers can be shaped and stretched into the image of Christ.

Eugene H. Peterson, long-time pastor and now a trainer of pastors, insightfully paraphrases the passage like this:

Christ handed out gifts of apostle, prophet, evangelist, and pastor-teacher to train Christians in skilled servant work, working within Christ's body, the church, until we're all moving rhythmically and easily with each other, efficient and graceful in response to God's Son, fully mature adults, fully developed within and without, fully alive in Christ. No prolonged infancies among us, please. . . Christ's very breath and blood flow through us, nourishing us so that we will grow up healthy in God, robust in love. [1]

God Wants Pastors Valued for Their Work's Sake

In 1 Thessalonians 5:12-13, Paul advises us, "We ask you, brothers, to respect those who work hard among you, who are over you in the Lord and who admonish you. Hold them in the highest regard in love because of their work. Live in peace with each other." Regarding this passage, New Testament scholar William Barclay explains, "The reason for the respect is the work the minister is doing. It is not a question of personal prestige; it is the task which makes a man great, and it is the service that he is doing that is his badge of honor." [2]

Though the organizational pattern between clergy and laypersons in the Thessalonian church is not known, Paul in the strongest language—some translations use words like *exhort* and *beseech*—calls the church to cherish its spiritual leaders for three reasons:

• Cherish them in love *for their work's sake.* Verse 12 says, "respect those who work hard among you." Authentic ministry, not for weaklings or shirkers, is hard, taxing work. Unlike the physical toil of a ditchdigger or carpet layer, this work requires listening to hurts, studying the Word, warning about sin, and never being free from people and their demands. Laypeople seldom experience such pressure.

This labor includes a pastor keeping his lip zipped when a lay leader sees him on the street at 10 P.M. and remarks what an easy life the pastor lives. That day the pastor was up at dawn to sit with a family while their father had cancer surgery, gave three hours to sermon preparation in the morning, chaired a finance subcommittee meeting at lunch, made six hospital calls in the afternoon, led a Bible study in the evening, and was now making a trip to the drugstore to get a prescription for a homebound parishioner.

• Cherish them in love *for their leadership in the Lord.* Pastoral leaders can lead like a CEO in a Fortune 500 company if they wish. But a minister's unique task is to keep folks connected to Christ in every dimension of their lives. The power of the pastor is spiritual authority that calls people to live continually under the lordship of Christ. This leadership is different from leadership in any other occupation and is best lived out as the minister invites his people "to come follow me as I follow Christ."

• Cherish them in love *who admonish you.* To admonish means to warn and instruct. Preaching and teaching are what matter most in the church. Like teaching a child not to cross a busy street, a pastor's admonition is not a mere safety lecture but a warning, "Keep out of the street! A car is coming!" The one who admonishes does not give take-it-or-leave-it advice. He communicates the meat of the Word of God which must be followed because it really matters. Peterson paraphrases "admonish" in verse 12 as "those who have been given responsibility for urging and guiding you along in your obedience."

After showing why spiritual leaders are so significant to the church, Paul urges us to, as one translation says, "Overwhelm them with appreciation and love!"

God Wants Followers to Follow

The Lord instructed Moses to send spies during the season of magnificent grapes to check out Canaan, a land God promised to give the Israelites (Num. 13:2). Their questions before the trip sound like those asked in many contemporary church decision meetings: Are the people strong or weak, few or many? Is the soil fertile or barren? Is there much fruit? Do they have many trees?

Forty days later the reports were given, accompanied by clusters of grapes that took two men to carry, not to mention the beautiful pomegranates and juicy figs. You remember the majority and minority report. Within a few verses of Scripture, the masses began grumbling against their leaders. They said they wished they had died in Egypt or out in the desert. They groused, "Let's choose a new leader who will take us back to Egypt." Listen to their silly rhetoric: "Wouldn't it be nice to choose a leader who would help us leave the Promised Land, take us back across the desert, have us cross the Red Sea in the opposite direction, and ask Pharaoh to enslave us again? We want a leader who will lead us in a backward retreat." Think of the lessons from this passage for today.

• *Realize you are blessed.* Like many contemporary congregations, the people of Israel didn't realize how blessed they were. They were closer to the Promised Land than they had ever been, though their situation was not perfect. But because they didn't have it all, they were ready to give up just as they stood on the edge of receiving the full benefit of God's promise.

• *Thank God for progress.* Avoid absurd notions about the good old days. Get realistic about current possibilities. No thinking person wants more slavery, bondage, deserts, Red Seas, and Pharaohs. There was nothing to go back to in Egypt. The kingdom's direction is always forward, but it is never to stay the same or regress. God's order is "Forward, march."

• *Resist a grasshopper complex.* Listen to the discouraging talk of the ten spies: "*We look like grasshoppers to the people of Canaan and to ourselves*" (v. 33). This inferiority complex is the epitome of a poor self-image. It's also a criticism of themselves as God's creation. Hundreds of contemporary churches are stymied because of a self-imposed grasshopper complex.

Every church can be more than it thinks. Every church leader can do more than he or she thinks. Teens are right when they say, "God doesn't make junk, and we are not junk." We are not some cosmic mistake. We have been providentially placed in this generation to do more than merely wait for the return of Jesus.

We have a message, a Gospel, and a lifestyle to proclaim to the world. There is no reason to be ashamed of what God planted, watered, and is bringing to fruition.

• *Stop grumbling.* When we view the account from Numbers, we see the leaders faced serious problems: "The whole assembly talked about stoning them" (14:10). Contemporary churches do the same thing but use different weapons. When groups resist accepting the will of God for their future, they usually grumble about leaders. They feel the need to blame someone, so they do. That's exactly what the people of Israel did. They wanted a new leader for the wrong reasons—they wanted to go back. They wanted to give up and miss the will of God. Think a long time before you murmur against your spiritual leader.

• *Refuse to convey a negative spirit.* Can you see the difference in Caleb's attitude? He said, "We should go up and take possession of the land, for we can certainly do it" (Num. 13:30). He sounds like a visionary pastor. But then the grumbling started: "They spread . . . a bad report about the land they had explored" (v. 32). Direct descendants of the doubters are still with us. They murmur in the vestibule, in the parking lot, and over the phone. Without realizing it, negative complainers spread a contagious spirit that keeps churches in the desert for years.

A negative spirit is like a deadly pollutant. Though it harms everyone, it usually hurts the one who expresses it most.

Note the lamentable results for the Israelites. The consequences went beyond anything they could have imagined. They and their children wandered around the desert for forty more years, with sand blowing in their hair, eyes, and teeth. They grumbled about how dangerous it was to go into the Promised Land without giving a thought to how dangerous it was to stay outside of it. They missed the Promised Land because of a negative spirit rooted in irrational fear. Many negative rumors could be eliminated if those who spread bad news faced their own anxieties.

• *Avoid poisonous humor.* The Israelites used sarcasm to reinforce their negative views. They joked, "Didn't we have enough graves in Egypt and the desert?" (Ex. 14:11) Like us, they found it easy to undermine the direction of God by using sick humor. It happens often in church decision groups.

In response, God wasn't the least bit amused when He asked Moses, "How long will these people treat Me with contempt? How long will they refuse to believe in Me, in spite of all the miraculous signs I have performed among them?" (Num. 14:11) When tempted to use derision and mockery in decision groups, lay leaders must examine themselves to see if their sarcasm is diverting the group's attention from what may really be the will of God.

• *Every decision requires energy and produces consequences.* Often a retreat requires as much or more energy as full speed ahead. It was especially true for the Children of Israel because most of their investment of energy took place long before Numbers 13 and 14. Without realizing it, we often try to do almost anything to avoid the risky adventures of fulfilling God's plans.

Obviously, few Israelites considered the possibility that they would wander around for forty more years before entering the Promised Land. Because of their delay, nearly two generations (if you count a generation as about twenty years) died before Israel entered the Promised Land. There are risks in moving ahead but there are consequences for delay. It is impossible to have one without the other.

• *Decisions must be viewed from how they look to God.* In discussing not going into the Promised Land, the complainers said almost nothing about the power of God to see them through. Complainers seldom factor God's power into their objections. Joshua and Caleb told the whole assembly, "The land we passed through and explored is exceedingly good. If the Lord is pleased with us, He will lead us into that land, a land flowing with milk and honey, and will give it to us. Only do not rebel against the Lord. And do not be afraid of the people of the land, because we will swallow them up. Their protection is gone, but the Lord is with us" (Num. 14:6-9). Regrettably, the crowd paid no attention and made no effort to view their situation from God's perspective. In fact, they wanted to kill the messengers.

God has always been faithful to His people, and He still is. He has brought us through dangers we didn't even see. How can church pillars turn back when they think about the power and promise of God? He promised the gates of hell will not prevail against the church. The battle is His. No weapon formed against us can prosper. Since we have His empowerment, we have no excuse for standing around the perimeters wondering whether He wills for us to move forward.

God is greater than the obstacles. The world needs the church now more than ever before. This means we must see our churches as powerful tools in the hands of God, much more than a little band of grasshoppers. Through the power of God, we can do everything He intends for us to do.

• *Human leaders need loyal followers.* Business management gurus say no one can be a leader who is not a follower. I wish we didn't make so many differences between leading and following. Ideally, they occur simultaneously in most of us. For example, I am a man, husband, father, grandfather, pastor, preacher, teacher, and writer. I can't completely sort the differences and distinctions, but I am all of these at the same time.

Leadership is like that too. I am a leader and follower, a teacher and learner. Often a leader does well to follow those he leads. Sometimes they know where the pleasant paths, quiet waters, and land mines are. In this account from Numbers, most Israelites chose to follow a fantasy leader who required no risks. Apparently a make-believe leader was more attractive to them than a flesh-and-blood person who said, "Let's move to the Promised Land" and reminded them that God would be with them. While avoiding the risk of moving forward, they experienced serious problems with staying where they were.

No leader can lead without loyal, faithful followers who commit to see that the church goes forward in fulfilling Christ's mission. Your pastor needs to hear you say, "We know God has given you dreams for this church. We thank God for your dreams. We're open for you to take us into the Promised Land. That's where we want to go." God, Moses, Joshua, and Caleb could not take the people where they did not want to go. Neither can your pastor.

• *Visions are easily clouded.* The Children of Israel could not see up close what they envisioned from afar. Apparently something happened on the way that corroded their dreams. Maybe the long journey dulled their vision. Maybe repetitive routines caused the loss. Maybe a declining passion for the ways of God clouded the vision. Maybe they convinced each other along the way to believe it could never happen. In any case, the vision was dull and dim and a distant hope.

Like a fire, a vision of Christ's mission has to be stirred and poked and refueled periodically in our hearts. The Israelites clearly teach us that we are beaten when we doubt. They demonstrate that if we say we can't, we won't. The vision, however, becomes bigger than life when we realize God works miracles through any effort we give Him. A clear vision produces an inner energy to go forward.

• *Influencers must use their influence.* In the record in Numbers, some of the people who influenced the decision to play it safe were not the most prominent leaders, but they still kept the people from entering the Promised Land. Those who created the greatest havoc are not even named in the passage, but they kept the group hostage to their doubts and fears.

It's the same today. Lay church pillars have lots of influence, sometimes much more than the pastor. Influencers often have been around for years, they know somebody, or they have money. Sometimes they are responsible for a yes or no vote even though they are not elected to a church office. While a pastor has been called by God, has years of experience, has been ordained, and has invested years in training for ministry, the person of influence may have more impact than the pastor about the church's future. Influence is an awesome responsibility that must be used with care.

Let's personalize this point. If you are a person of influence in your church, you may determine whether the church goes into the Promised Land, stays in the desert, or goes back to Egypt. Though influencers sometimes block innovation and change, they don't often offer alternative plans. That's the flip side of misused influence. One who blocks moving into the Promised Land bears responsibility for lack of progress, dimmed vision, and spiritual and numerical decline. What a frightening responsibility to keep a whole generation living and dying on the edge of the desert when they were so near the Promised Land. Be careful you don't die a few steps from it.

Positively using your influence may involve some risks, but staying in the desert and longing for Egypt has risks too. The contemporary church may be just a few feet away from the Promised Land, so why choose to die in the desert?

God Wants Spiritually Authentic Lay Leaders

Some years ago Fletcher Spruce published a list of spiritual qualities of laypersons called "Fine Lines for Laymen (Kansas City, Mo.: Beacon/Standard n.d.)," based on 1 Timothy 3. Here is the list:

• *Bite your tongue* (v. 8). Some people talk so much it appears they are double-tongued. John Wesley suggested that it is impossible to hold a conversation more than thirty minutes without saying something that shouldn't be said. Think about that.

• *Watch your priorities* (v. 8). "Not pursuing dishonest gain" means that work, saving, and accumulation are not the highest priority. Are you being kicked to death by the golden calf? The test of prosperity may be more difficult than the test of adversity.

• *Keep free from addictions* (v. 8). This verse warns about wine, but other addictions kill a layperson's service too, like tobacco, drugs, prescription medicine, food, and gossip.

• *Cultivate radiant religion* (v. 9). *The Living Bible* translates the passage, ". . . earnest, wholehearted followers of Christ who is the hidden Source of their faith." The religion lay leaders need is not the kind of faith that leaves you cold, with an anemic witness and a cloudy conscience. Calvary's fountain can wash away frustrations, guilt complexes, and the twisting tensions of life and bring you the beauty of Christlikeness. Keep the awe, the wonder, the breathless adoration of the Savior in your heart.

• *Take faith home with you* (v. 12). Good religion works at home as well as in church. A well-managed household is required for a pillar in the church.

• *Be faithful in all things* (v. 11). That's the mark of righteous people. They are so dependable that they will come to church in stormy weather, stand by the pastor even when he makes a mistake, pay their tithe as sure as they make their mortgage payments, and take their witnessing into the marketplace. Scripture is right: they "gain a good standing for themselves and also great confidence in the faith which is in Christ Jesus" (v. 13, RSV).

God Wants Double Honor

A time like ours, when pastors are giving up in droves and fresh recruits are slower to join up, provides an excellent opportunity for us to rethink and revolutionize our ideas about pastoral relationships. This is a good time to multiply affirmation for the minister of the church we attend and lead. Consider the Apostle Paul's double honor idea. He said, "Elders who direct the affairs of the church well are worthy of double honor, especially those whose work is preaching and teaching" (1 Tim. 5:17).

What the Playbook Says

Did you hear the passage? Double honor, according to Paul, goes to those who direct the affairs of the church by their preaching and teaching. Though biblical scholars have some disagreement about the precise meaning of "double honor," it has to mean a lot more than the honor many churches give their pastors now. Whether the command is for money or affection, most ministers could use a lot more of both. I read the passage in several translations and consulted enough commentaries to know it means giving pastors abundant honor for their work and paying them as generously as possible.

Barclay summarizes, "The minister whom the church really honored was to be the minister who worked to edify and build up the church by his preaching of truth to people, and his educating of the young and the new converts in the Christian way."[3] Much of a pastor's effectiveness or ineffectiveness will be due to whether lay leaders cherish or disdain his work. In 1 Timothy 5:17-25, Paul refers to the church's attitude and action regarding a minister's salary, discipline, and worthiness of character. All these concerns are impacted by lay leaders who make or mar a minister's ministry.

Author Paul Barackman shines a bright light of reality on the honor issue:

> It is a fact that except for those in high places, servants of the church have never been provided for with much generosity. The church of Jesus Christ may well be proud, and humbled as well, that through the years so many dedicated men and women have borne privation of this world's goods that they might minister to the church. Ability to preach and teach the gospel is a gift not found every day. It deserves to be valued more highly than it is.[4]

Try giving your pastor double honor. Be careful, because the double honor idea may shock her at first. Give your pastor more encouragement, more support, more friendship, and more money because he needs it and because it is the right thing to do. Speak well of your pastor; pray for him and believe him to be a holy person before God. A church that doesn't honor its pastor will likely never become a genuine New Testament church.

Doubling and tripling love for your pastor might produce several wonderful surprises. A church that cherishes its leader often prospers in several tangible ways:

• A fulfilled pastor works harder with more loving motivation; as a result, she shares more inspiration and spiritual energy with the church family.

• Soon a church will reflect the new perspective of the pastor; as leader, he helps set the tone either positively or negatively.

• Church pillars have the joy of seeing their pastor fulfilled and the church prospering.

• God can be expected or perhaps He may even be obligated to bless a church that does everything possible to keep its pastor spiritually, physically, and emotionally healthy.

The time has come for every church to reevaluate and reenergize its pastoral relationship. It's time to strengthen ministers everywhere. The church can't get along without them, and we don't want to try.

Let's come alongside the man or woman of God—to lift with him, to pray with him, to sacrifice with him. Cherish him for his work's sake. Pray for his spiritual prosperity. Thank God every time you think about him. In this confusing epoch of human history, God wants His church strong and valiant; that can't happen without spiritually vibrant shepherds. The Head of the church wants every pastor loved into greatness, encouraged into nobility, and inspired into making God's will a delightful reality for themselves and the church. Pastors need your support, affirmation, and love. Why not with all your heart give your pastor what he needs and longs for?

When pastors succeed spiritually, they will lead us into the spiritual and social revolution that our world needs.

RENEWAL STRATEGIES FOR CHURCH PILLARS
Follow What the Playbook Says

1. Honor your pastor for his work's sake.

2. Cherish your pastor's admonitions.

3. Realize your church is blessed in many ways.

4. Resist a grasshopper mentality.

5. Stop grumbling.

6. Be faithful in all things.

7. Avoid poisonous humor.

8. Realize dreams are fragile.

9. Challenge influencers to use their influence for good.

10. Scrutinize your priorities.

"The church Christ is building is His. It does not belong to the members; they belong to Him. It does not belong to the officers; they belong to Him. It does not belong to the pastor; the pastor belongs to Him. It does not belong to a hierarchy; the hierarchy belongs to Him....Wherever the church is, it belongs to Jesus Christ alone."

Richard Halverson

3. WHAT PASTORS WISH CONGREGATIONS KNEW ABOUT MINISTRY

Applying the Golden Rule to Leading

Make us sturdy pillars in Your church, O God.
Help us discover a God-fearing perspective that is
. . . accurate with Scripture,
. . . attuned to present day needs,
. . . transforming for sinners,
. . . fulfilling to our minister,
. . . satisfying to those who worship here,
and may it be especially pleasing to Your dear will.
Let Your grace grow in us. May this body of believers be what You
want rather than what we want. Amen.

Being a pastor and a lay leader in the church are vastly different positions. Pastor and lay leader need to realize how enormous these differences are and that neither will be able to fully understand the other's perspective. In spite of encouraging signs that a lay ministry movement seems to be developing—a wonderful revolution—there are still essential differences in intensity, training, perspective, and viewpoint that must be accepted with charity and grace.

In many informal conversations, both of us have asked pastors what they wish their congregations and lay leaders knew about ministry. Several dilemmas surface over and over again. When they are understood and discussed, many of these issues can be "aha" moments in relationships between ministers and church leaders. Several of the most common frustrations follow.

51

Your Pastor Is an Endangered Species

Criticism Stings

Criticism wounds pastors, a fact some lay leaders find hard to understand. They ask why the minister can't be more thick-skinned. They wonder why a pastor feels troubled when one person criticizes or complains while politicians are satisfied with a 51 percent approval rating.

What appears to be oversensitivity develops in ministers because their commitments link them so completely with what happens in the church. Often they view themselves as organizational lightning rods that attract approval or disapproval. Thus, criticism to a pastor, often sounds like a rebuff or insult. Recently, our pastor put the matter into clear focus when he said, "Your pastoral team will make mistakes, but our heart is right. We want to do right."

Such a response may be easier to understand when we recall how often pastors are called upon to represent God in so many ways at so many events for so many years. In their minds some are never free from this burden. As a result, ministers, without meaning to do so, begin thinking critics are whining against God when they offer suggestions about the church or its programs. Right or wrong, ministers tend to internalize criticism of the church, members of the congregation, or members of their family.

The root of this sensitivity is explained by Dr. Rodney Hunter, professor of pastoral theology at Candler School of Theology at Emory University in Atlanta. He commented, "Ministry is a complex undertaking because it stimulates and focuses on the minister the deeply ambivalent feelings people have about God, authority, and life."[1] If Hunter is right, when a pastor hears criticism, he thinks something more significant and deep-seated is likely taking place. And he may be right.

In church life criticism often comes in two ways—as a helpful reaction to a mistake or oversight, or as unfair condemnation. When criticism comes in a helpful way, it is often accepted or even welcomed; then, the one offering the comment is seen as having the best interests of the pastor or congregation in mind. But when criticism sounds like a bad-spirited complaint, it is quickly rejected as harmfully antagonistic; the one criticizing is considered to be contentious. Such a critic undercuts a pastor's need for self-respect and approval.

Since difficult dynamics, as we have seen, are at work in giving and receiving criticism, disapproval should be avoided if possible. However, when it is given, it must be with an affirming attitude at the right time with the right words. Those who study these matters say six filters immediately go into play when criticism is given or received:

1. Feelings about one's worth.
2. Sensitivity to recognized inadequacies.
3. Blurred targets.
4. Prior experiences with disapproval.
5. An evaluation of the setting where criticism is given.
6. An assessment of the intentions of persons involved.[2] When voicing and hearing criticism, the persons involved should be ready to face all of these filters simultaneously.

Try to protect your pastor from criticism, or do your best to quiet the uproar when others complain. One experienced lay leader was right on when he observed, "In the church, one Nervous Nellie or Ned stirring up criticism does as much damage as a careless mechanic spilling gasoline on a hot engine." Avoid Nellie's or Ned's tactics as you avoid the plague. Keep reminding yourself that many keen observers of the contemporary church believe as much as half the problems come from criticism started by misinformed people. On the contrary, it is wise to remember that what is frequently called criticism is nothing more than people talking about preferences.

Try doubling your affirmation of your pastor and watch the result. Cut criticism in half. Remember, many church complaints aren't really significant—they simply mean someone wants to be heard. One wise veteran churchman observed, "There are three reasons for talk and gossip: some people want information, some want to use information, but most want to talk about it."

Probably about 85 percent of criticism is recreational talk; but the remaining 15 percent should be used to help you keep growing and loving and attracting others to the Gospel. Robert Frost gave advice that works well in the church: Love what's lovable and hate what's hate-able—it takes brains to know the difference.[3]

As a lay leader, commit yourself to fix that which can be fixed. But beyond that, criticism should be viewed as trifling, and you must expect people to talk about those who lead. Jesus' advice on the matter: "Blessed are the peacemakers, for they will be called the sons of God" (Matt. 5:9).

Meanwhile, let's join Christian psychologist Paul Meier and his colleagues in expressing appreciation to pastors who serve so well on the front line: "You, dear Pastor, are vital to every one of us in the Christian community. For some reason—perhaps because we are human too—we are quicker to criticize you for what you aren't doing than to thank you for what you are doing. It's unfortunate and unfair, because you deserve many heartfelt thank-yous."[4]

Conflict Is Inevitable

Lay leaders, like pastors, must face the fact that conflict is almost inevitable whenever people come together in groups. Check the Bible; conflict has been around since the patriarchs. Ministers live with controversy most of the time, but it can be used creatively. Thus, they need lay leaders to understand a pastor can't take sides in a disagreement even when he has strong opinions about the issues. And to uncomplicate things, ministers often wish lay leaders would not create unnecessary conflict just to keep things stirred. Save your ammunition for big stuff.

Regrettably, conflict sometimes originates from reasonably unimportant issues, such as budgeting, carpet color, schedules for Sunday services, music worship styles, choice of visiting preachers, and a thousand other small details. Conflict may also arise when inappropriate behavior or unbecoming attitudes must be challenged; then the challenger is sometimes viewed as the problem.

Some controversies, however, can be constructive. The choice is to intentionally use conflict or to do nothing, and allow a congregational deadlock. Consider the positive possibilities that might come from conflict management: controversies can help clarify issues, help potential solutions emerge, and provide a way to move toward a resolution of differences. Conflict can be useful as leaders confront each other honestly, consider each other's viewpoints, listen to each other's positions, and seek to make decisions that will unify the body of Christ.

Try not to put yourself or your pastor into an emotional and administrative straitjacket by acting as if conflict and controversy do not exist. Conflict is a fact of congregational life which can be used creatively or even redemptively. The alternative is to allow conflict to divide a church and scatter the flock.

Pastoring Is a Way of Life, Not a Job

Everyone has heard the unrealistic joke about a minister's easy job— "He only works one day a week." In ensuing banter, pastors sometimes protest, a non-clergy person comes to the defense of the minister, or sometimes this inane humor dies in midair. It's actually sadistic humor.

Let's look at the bigger vocational landscape. Outside church vocations, the world of work is often divided into professions, positions, jobs, and business owners. The ministry is like each of these categories because it requires skill, knowledge, talent, and strength, but it is also different from all the others too. Pastoral work requires a whole person, body, soul, and spirit. Like law, medicine, or education, ministry necessitates specialized preparation and commitment to one constituency. Just as if he held a position in a corporation, a minister works for the church, is paid without punching a time clock, is free to perform tasks according to his priorities, and is expected to contribute significantly to the common good. Like a job, ministry involves clearly defined tasks that must be accomplished in a timely manner at a specific location for an organization that pays a salary. Then, like a small business owner, a pastor must pay attention to financial stability and the care of facilities if the church is to run smoothly.

But there is more. Ministry is a way-of-life proposition for a whole person. As Pastor Milo Arnold explained,

> Engineers may be chosen for their skills in one line of work, while their moral lives may be corrupt and their social lives base. Musicians may be chosen for their ability to make music, whether they can make a life or not. Farmers may raise crops which will feed the world without having the least sense of inner loftiness. Builders may erect houses without being qualified in the least as persons. And attorneys may effectively represent oth-

ers at the law while violating the laws of God. But when God calls a minister, there must be a real person. He must be through and through a Christian.[5]

Your pastor wants you to realize pastoral ministry is different from any of the other four occupational categories. Just as the church is a unique force in our society, the minister is God's unique person. Ministry has several unique factors that interact with each other. A pastor is on call twenty-four hours *every* day—he must be available. The minister's character affects his service. The pastor carries eternal responsibility for those under his care. His marriage affects his ministry. The pastor's work goes forward best through a whole network of solid people relationships. The minister also uses specialized tools. While others use calculators, hammers, computers, or blueprints, the minister uses prayer, Scripture, and love to mold those who use them. Unlike any other line of work, the vigor and purity of a pastor's inner life determines the quality of ministry.

It's important to remember your pastor has been trusted by God and the congregation to lead your church. She is not an employee nor hireling. Though persons do not come to a pastor with broken machines or wounded bodies, they bring sin-scarred souls. They come with marred lives, broken spirits, and damaged emotions. They come hoping God will assist with their pressing needs. And a minister does something amazingly different from other employees. He introduces them to Jesus Christ, whom to know is life eternal (John 17:3).

Every Pastor Requires Spiritual Care

Every Christian knows a church's zeal and stamina are largely dependent on a pastor's spiritual vitality. On this issue it is not difficult to get a hardy amen from both clergy and laity. When the rhetoric gets stripped away, the clear reality is that we can't revolutionize the church if we cannot find ways to help pastors keep growing spiritually. Having talked about the need for spiritual strength in our shepherd, we usually go about our business without doing anything about it. Creativity, commitment, and priority are needed to see that it happens.

What Pastors Wish Congregations Knew about Ministry

Ministry, to borrow Eugene H. Peterson's term, has become spiritually undercapitalized. Symptoms of frightening spiritual bankruptcy show in contemporary churches when more ministry is attempted than the spiritual resources can support adequately. Then a church runs on empty, her spiritual balances stand near zero, and her credit card of character is maxed out.

Then, doing becomes more important than being; knowing more important than serving. Tragically, without some serious infusion of spiritual capital, we will face more spiritually bankrupt churches and more spiritually jeopardized ministers. The current ecclesiastical landscape is strewn with many shocking examples of bankrupt churches and spiritually compromised pastors.

Can we find some remedy or prevention? As a quantum forward leap, lay leaders need to recognize that no church can be spiritually healthy when its leaders are spiritually shallow or drained. Then church pillars, to keep spiritual bankruptcy from taking place, must encourage pastors to keep spiritually fit and keep themselves spiritually strong at the same time.

Persuade your minister to take time away from the routine to grow his own soul. Give your pastor a book allowance so he can keep current and read the devotional greats. Urge him to take one-day retreats on a quarterly basis for prayer and reflection. Key lay leaders should be asked to talk with the pastor about what additional resources he needs to keep spiritually fit: is it time, budget, inspiration, or encouragement? Try to meet every reasonable request. Often such a friendly discussion about a pastor's concerns helps a minister refocus on the main issues of his spiritual health.

Do your church a gigantic favor by finding ways to resource your pastor so he can keep in spiritual shape. Like physical conditioning, spiritual fitness is never automatic, but it is among the most vital ingredients of congregational well-being.

Though spiritual self-care is an absolute necessity and responsibility for the minister, every congregation, through its lay leaders, can encourage a pastor to grow spiritually strong. When a pastor withers spiritually, it takes a terrible toll on everyone.

Pastors Need a Middle-class Paycheck

An increasing number of pastors feel pinched by not being able to keep up economically. In most churches in North America, pastors are expected to live at a middle-class standard in their dress, transportation, home furnishings, and the repayment of educational loans, to say nothing about their children's college expenses. Except for the reasonably well-paid pastors in middle or larger churches, most pastors' wages are not adequate to cover family needs. In many situations, the spouse's outside income is what makes it possible for the pastor to continue in ministry.

When pastors get together, they say they wish lay leaders knew more about pastoral money matters. It would be so helpful if some responsible lay leaders asked periodically about this issue. When a church does all it can to be fair about a pastor's compensation, that should be enough. But the heartbreaking frustration for pastors comes from churches where pastoral support is placed lowest in the congregation's economic priorities. More than anyone cares to admit, pastors often feel forced to move to another church because they are overwhelmed with personal financial problems in their present setting.

Think clearly about this issue. Would you want your pastor to move to another church to receive more financial support when your congregation has funds in the bank, or ministry dollars still in church members' pockets? In the care and feeding of pastors, money talks about how much a congregation really cares for its ministry family.

Preaching Takes Time and Soul-agony

Contrary to what some non-preachers think, effective preaching takes hard work, emotional effort, and soul-searching. A few pastors have a natural preaching gift, but even those special gifts get ministers nowhere if they do not continually sharpen their skills. Those who appear to be the most gifted are usually the ones who have spent long hours getting ready for a specific sermon and who have kept paying the price for effective preaching for years.

Anyone who has ever preached knows one can get by with minimum effort. But preaching that lifts and loves and challenges folks takes time, meditation, musing, and pondering. Words from Pastor

What Pastors Wish Congregations Knew about Ministry

Daniel Walker turn the spotlight on this issue:

Some time ago I visited a large Protestant church and heard the senior minister preach. Tall and handsome, he was a commanding figure in the pulpit. He had a fine voice and was obviously sincere. But his sermon missed the mark. It wasn't bad. It wasn't good. It was organized, but it wasn't well organized. It was intelligent, but it wasn't moving. Based clearly on Scripture, it was relevant to our time, yet it could not be defined as inspired utterance. It had no power. *I am confident no one left the service that day feeling he had been struck with the fist of a righteous God or lifted into the arms of a loving Father.* . . . Neither the pastor nor his laymen believed sufficiently in preaching to see that it had first place in his life and his commitments, not only on Sunday, but every day of the week.[6]

Sermons that come from God do more than soothe folks. Real sermons make a difference in someone's life, like helping those who drift find their way, helping the fearful find courage, helping the doubter discover crystal-clear faith, helping the grieving find comfort, helping the wavering recover fortitude, and helping the depressed feel the warm sun of God's grace again.

Church pillars must recognize that effective preaching takes time and that it belongs high in a congregation's priorities. Thinking, seeking, praying, stretching, and preparing are all part of preaching's time-consuming necessities. Of course, preaching requires as much preparation as any good speech. But it also requires the wonderful, terrible agony of drawing close enough to God for the preacher to be convinced his sermon is the Lord's message for his congregation at this time.

Pillars can encourage good preaching by informing the congregation about the pastor's usual time for study and asking people to respect those times. Lay leaders, by asking a few leading questions, can find out what a pastor needs to help her preach better; maybe it is space for study, or equipment, or a book budget. One church argued for years about whether or not a small wall heater was needed in the

59

pastor's study, while another church argued through a whole summer about purchasing a small window air conditioner for the pastor's study. Another church board had controversy for months over the need for a new computer in the pastor's study. Let's get sensible about such issues. If a pastor is too cold, too hot, or needs a computer, it is in the congregation's interest to provide what she needs.

As we listen to ministers in pastors' conferences, it appears the things they need most to help them preach better are more time, more books, and a comfortable space that is conducive to authentic intercession, serious study, and thoughtful reflection. Pastor Robert Hudnut puts this need in focus: "Each week it is the preacher alone with the Bible. It is what comes out of the preacher's aloneness that counts."[7] For some unknown reason, a setting that encourages listening, aloneness, and quiet stillness is difficult for many pastors to find. Every church should assist its pastor to have such a place so the congregation may hear the Word of God preached more effectively through the lips, the heart, and mind of the man or woman of God who is their pastor.

Crisis Care Drains Pastors

Every pastor, even in the smallest church, deals with many crises in people's lives. If anybody, even those with casual church connection, seeks pastoral care, it will be during times of pain and transition. However, many of those crises are so confidential a pastor can never discuss them. That is why a minister may show frightening signs of emotional fatigue that no one understands, not even his family.

Think of the problems a pastor faces with people. One church with fewer than 100 members presented the following crises to their pastor in one week—not a typical week, but not especially unusual either. Though not all of these problems came from active members, each person had some connection with the church and wanted the pastor to minister to him or her. And that, of course, is what he wanted to do. Here's the list. John and Sally are considering a divorce, the third time this year. Mary Ruth, age seventy-five, wants to know if God will forgive her for an abortion she had forty-five years ago. Tim and Sue are desperate with worry about finding money to send their daughter to a Christian college. Molly, age five, drowned this week, and the pastor wept with her family and conducted her funeral; she was the same age as his youngest daughter. Meanwhile, Dan and Roberta grieve over their sixteen-year-old daughter, who left home last week; they have no idea where she is. Think of the incredible spiritual and emotional stamina a pastor needs for dealing with such a demanding accumulation of problems in one week.

Pastors Want Ministry to Matter to You

Every pastor had a living encounter with Christ at some point in their past that set him apart for ministry. That call was so life-changing that it motivated your pastor to sign on for a holy partnership with God to help change the world through the church. It's awesome to realize a person like that stands in the pulpit of your church each Sunday pleading with you to be like Christ and showing you how.

In spite of the serious commitment of their pastors, many churches show signs of widespread superficiality. Attendance at church dinners and balancing the budget seem more important than transformed lives. Church membership has often been trivialized into an expression of congregational preference rather than Christian commitment and do or die covenant. Consumer mentality is everywhere in contemporary culture, including the church, so unsatisfied people switch churches; a family in our town changed churches because the parking lot was too congested. Gloomy, discouraged attitudes among faithful attenders are common. Many churches and believers lack what first-century Christians possessed in such abundant measure—a wholehearted, Christ-centered faith that produced unspeakable personal joy.

Yet, many contemporary nonchurch people, without knowing what to call it, feel homesick for what the early church possessed and shared in faith, commitment, obedience, meaning, and assurance. Contemporary people are learning that secular values cannot make good on their promise. If the church gets to the place where faith is again the most valuable thing in the lives of her people, it will require a holy conspiracy between pastors and serious laymen to pay whatever price it takes to kindle renewal and revival.

Your Pastor Is an Endangered Species

That's what your pastor dreamed about accomplishing when he was called into the ministry. It's what mattered then, and it's what matters to many ministers now. Let's pray and believe—lay leaders and pastors—for an authentic renewing of the church so it can revolutionize the world for Christ.

Deep down, every pastor longs for such a moving of God in her personal pilgrimage as well as in the life of the congregation. Dare to commit yourself to be one God can use to bring about renewal in your church. The needed renewal must start in our hearts. What we long to see will come when we start loving like Christ loved. As a church pillar, help your pastor's deepest longing become a reality in your life, your family, your church, your community, and your world.

Ministry and Marriage Are Always Tied Together

For most of this century, congregations assumed when they called a pastor they would have two people for the price of one, getting the spouse free. At the same time, pastors and spouses have believed marriage and ministry are inevitably in rivalry. To make pastoral relationships more realistic and rewarding, both notions need to be overhauled.

To a congregation, there is a given in a pastor's marital status: calling a pastor to serve a church means marriage and family are part of the proposition. It's inevitable. This is even true of an unmarried clergyman—his singleness will affect his ministry and how people view his service. In each case, whether the impact turns out positive or negative depends on how all parties view the realities.

Several agreements about the minister's family should be made between congregational pillars and their pastors. Ideally, these discussions should be held at the beginning of a pastorate, but they can be reviewed and implemented at any point along the journey together:

1. Don't expect perfection of the pastor's family.
2. Families are unique and should not be expected to be like any other family.
3. A pastor should be encouraged to give time, effort, and energy to life-long development of his marriage

and family. Every pastor functions better when things are going well at home.

4. Should your pastor be a workaholic, encourage him to set weekly time blocks for marriage and family.

5. Resist words like, "Our former pastor's family did it differently than you do."

6. Befriend the pastor's family with the same warmth you show other new people or old friends in your church.

7. The pastor's family needs a surrogate extended family—uncles, aunts, and grandparents.

8. Don't expect the pastor's spouse or children to play the piano, head a highly visible ministry, or shoot a pistol.

9. Expect the family to grieve over leaving their last church; the process can't be rushed.

10. Offer them massive affection and affirmation.

Inasmuch as the pastor's family is such a vital part of the minister's life, church pillars should make every effort to meet the needs of the family. As a church, work to be worthy of the full backing of spouse and children; it's an important ingredient in a pastor's fulfillment. Pay attention to the children. Adjust needed details in the housing arrangements—small but worthwhile investments in ministry to your congregation. We (Neil and Bonnie) were once forced to live with ugly linoleum in a parsonage kitchen because it was two dollars cheaper per yard than what we really liked. (In that small kitchen it was an eight-dollar difference.) Though the decision-makers never realized it, how we felt was worth significantly more than the cost difference.

No Pastor Chooses Burnout

Burnout is increasing among pastors these days. It is caused by too much stress carried for too long without relief. Several factors built into ministry contribute to this problem, the greatest being no one pays much attention to symptoms of tiredness, boredom, or withdrawal.

The most obvious drain on spiritual and emotional energy comes from working with troubled or dysfunctional people. On the surface, the energy investment seems unimportant because so little physical energy is used in this process. But when a minister remarked how tired he was, a neighboring minister said, "How many spiritual blood transfusions can you give in a week without becoming sick yourself?"

Perpetual unfinished work is another potential burnout factor. A carpenter completes a job before he starts a new one. An auto mechanic fixes one car before starting on another. But unlike these tradespeople, a pastor is never finished—there is always something left undone. As a lay leader, you should question your pastor about his long hours. Gently insist that your pastor put a limit on his work week. Nudge him to follow the scriptural teaching regarding taking a day for rest and renewal.

Unclear ways of evaluating ministry is another burnout factor. Athletes see a scoreboard. Physicians see patients get well. Businessmen check profit statements. Construction workers point to a house they built. But ministers rarely realize the extent of their influence on people. A former parishioner called a few days ago to tell me how much my ministry impacted him twenty years ago—I always wondered.

The repetitive factors of ministry likewise contribute to pastoral burnout. Psychologist John A. Sanford explains, "Repetitive work loses its creativity. The first number of times we perform a certain function it may bring us energy, but eventually we wear out the creativity of the work because we have repeated it so often. Exhaustion and boredom are the inevitable result."[8] In a minister's work, there are many repetitive tasks, such as preaching, counseling, administration, and hospital calls.

You can almost feel the powerful agony in author Lloyd Rediger's summary of burnout causes: "Burnout happens when a pastor gives away so much of him/herself that he/she cannot fulfill ministry any longer."[9] Of course, your pastor would like lay leaders to realize that the potential of burnout is a continuous risk for ministers.

Though they may not show it, pastors need lay leaders to be aware of the causes of burnout, to watch them for signs of it, to give them permission to avoid burnout, and to initiate the recovery process when the problem begins to show.

The best prevention any pastor can have is found in spiritual resources. This connection is insightfully described by Eugene H. Peterson: "I do not find the emaciated, exhausted spirituality of institutional careerism adequate. I do not find the veneered, cosmetic spirituality of personal charisma adequate. I require something biblically spiritual—rooted and cultivated in creation and covenant, leisurely in Christ, soaked in Spirit."[10]

Opinions Aren't Final

Too often pastors and lay leaders paint themselves into a corner by expressing opinions as if they were facts that cannot be changed. Nearly everyone sometimes changes his mind, and the rest of us wish we could and still save face. It's easy to say more than we mean; as the old hill woman suggested, "It's sure easy to over-speak." For everyone's benefit, help your pastor create a climate in your church decision group where it is easy to say, "I have been thinking a lot about what I said at our last meeting, and I think there may be another way to look at this issue." Create an administrative atmosphere where anyone is free to say, "I have gained more insight." "I have more information." "I was having a bad day when I made that last speech." Or "I was wrong."

Some strong lay leaders find it nearly impossible to change their mind or to allow anyone else to rethink a position. Pastors sometimes experience the same problem. But let's get our perspective more accurate by remembering we are frail children of the creative God who seems to use us even when we are weak and know it. Thus, when your decision group seems to be at an impasse, it is best to let a question simmer. Some controversial issues completely die that way. Others are restudied later with new vigor and with willingness to consider alternative solutions.

In your attempt not to be overly brittle about your church work, try to remember the advice of the late Bishop Gerald Kennedy of the United Methodist Church: "You can't take out of a person's mind with reason what reason did not put into it in the first place."[11] An insightful sentence from Jan Linn further clarifies this issue, "Reason may help, but reason alone will not change people's minds." Often church members believe something because of how they feel, what they fear, or what they hope never changes. Anyone who leads in the church needs to try to understand what makes people think and act the way they do. People need to be accepted for what they are. God is at work remaking us all into the image of Christ. And that takes more time for some than others.

Allow people to change, grow, and mature. Cheerfully give them room to rethink their position. Allow that flexibility for your pastor and practice it for yourself. Then the church will be more loving and accepting, with less strife and less division. That's the kind of church every pastor longs to serve.

Healthy Churches Focus on Outreach

Most churches in North America average fewer than 100 people in attendance. While many of these churches are alive and well and make a vital contribution to kingdom efforts, some have allowed themselves to become ingrown, judgmental, and legalistic. This usually happens when the church focuses inward rather than outward. The solution is to focus ministry on the needs of persons outside the church.

I Wish I Knew Someone Prayed for Me

It gives a pastor incredible strength and encouragement when he knows someone prays for him. Too often we feel our need for a pastor to pray for us, forgetting how much the man or woman of God needs our prayers.

Here's a sample prayer to stimulate your praying for your minister:

Dear God, bless my pastor today!
Make him too big to be little, too wise to be foolish, too holy to be selfish, too spiritual to be worldly, too tall to get a chip on his shoulder, too dedicated to swerve, too zealous to be idle, too noble to be coarse, too happy to be morbid.
Save him from the love of big words, the fear of worldly people, the tedium of too many announcements.
Deliver him from the rut of preaching too long, the pit of pointless preaching, the evil of emotionless messages.
Strengthen him when the tempter would lure him into sins shal-

low or deep, when the stand he must take will not be appreciated by the people who help pay his salary, when he is the target of gossiping tongues.

Empower him with the Holy Spirit to make him strong in the pulpit, with the Spirit of Christ to make him calm under pressure, with the spirit of joy to make him strong even in weakness.

Keep him from toning down the biblical message to please the worldly, from trimming down his sermons into sermonettes, from talking down to his congregation (Fletcher Spruce).

RENEWAL STRATEGIES FOR CHURCH PILLARS
How the Situation Looks to Your Pastor

1. Realize criticism hurts even though it may be true.

2. Accept conflict as a price of progress.

3. Promote the understanding that ministry is a way of life, not a job.

4. Be sure your pastor gets personal spiritual care.

5. Push for middle-class pay for your pastor.

6. Respect the hard toil preaching requires.

7. Understand how crisis pastoral care drains ministers.

8. Tell your pastor how important his ministry is to your spiritual development.

9. Remember a minister's ministry and marriage are closely tied together.

10. Treat pastoral burnout as a preventable illness.

*"Do You want my hands,
Lord, to spend the day helping the sick and the poor
who need them? Lord,
today I give You my hands.
"Do You want my feet,
Lord, to spend the day visiting those who need a
friend? Lord, today
I give You my feet.
"Do You want my voice,
Lord, to spend the day
speaking to all who need
Your words of love? Lord,
today I give You my voice.
"Do You want my heart,
Lord, to spend the day loving everyone without excep-
tion? Lord, today I give You
my heart."*

Mother Teresa

4. OVERCOMING THE MYTHS
Creating Strong Bonds Between Pastors and Pillars

Lord of the church, empower us to
> *. . . see past the myths that blind us,*
> *. . . overlook differences that divide us,*
> *. . . suspect sentiments that sandpaper us,*
> *. . . intercede for the pastor who leads us,*
> *. . . seek the righteousness You promised us,*
>   *so we may lovingly win those who have lost their way. Amen.*

"Many unexamined religious assumptions can't be discussed with lay persons" was the conclusion a beginning minister—let's call him Pastor McWilliams—shared with his pastoral mentor. He continued, "These notions drive me crazy."

To encourage additional discussion, the older minister—let's call him Pastor Adams—acted as if he did not understand. So McWilliams continued to argue his point vehemently. "If I were a doctor, I could discuss any symptoms with my patients. Then we would make a diagnosis, find a remedy, and hopefully get them back on the road to health. But I'm supposed to be the physician of my parishioners' souls, and I can't even discuss many issues with them. It seems people would rather keep pain in their soul or debilitating illness in the church than seek a solution. It's frustrating. Layer upon layer of old ways of thinking, notions or practices that don't make sense keep pastors

71

and parishioners from developing a common dream for their future together. If we could talk about it, many undiscussed taboos would entirely evaporate."

Desiring to direct the young McWilliams' reactions toward some resolution, Pastor Adams replied, "Maybe someone should write a chapter in a book for lay leaders about those issues."

Adams was right, and that is what this chapter is about.

Myth #1—Problems Get Smaller with Silence

"I don't want to talk about it."

Denying problems in the church is like closing our eyes to symptoms of a disease. Left alone long enough, the disease can be lethal. Think of what untreated diseases cause: chronic discomfort, acute pain, loss of motor and/or mental skills, or death.

The same is true with destructive symptoms in churches. Problems must be solved. Saying "I don't see a problem at the church," or "I don't want to talk about it" never helps.

As an example, consider the troubles a financial shortfall causes. The problem, when ignored, creates persistent pain, so some ministry areas are shortchanged, crippled, or even eliminated. When funds are cut, a less obvious but harmful problem results because people who serve in those ministries lose motivation or settle for minimum effort. Continuous underfunding hurts the cause, turns neglected maintenance into major repairs, or dries up giving for missions.

Many people who advocate delayed action do not consider that ignored problems never go away; instead, they usually get bigger. No action usually means low courage, not knowing a method for correcting the difficulty, or a lack of will to act. In any case, the church suffers and the pastor lives with unending frustration over dreams of what might have been.

Or think about a moral failure in a church leader. It does not go away because it is ignored; delay simply makes matters worse. Neither does the gossip virus lose its damaging effect just because it is ignored; in fact, some churches gossip about gossip.

Action, remedy, and possibly surgery are ways an effective doctor deals with a fever or infection. He knows the difference between a scratch on the thumb and a tumor on the brain. A scratch can heal naturally, but a tumor demands immediate attention. In either case, a decision must be made about how to deal with the problem. In its decision processes, the church needs forthrightness.

Certainly, pushing problems into a mental closet and pretending they do not exist solves nothing. Denial offers no remedies. Pretending doesn't help either. Everyone realizes that problems exist in any human organization, including the church. Thus, problems need to be identified and solved. Forgiveness needs to be given and received. Correctives need to be implemented. And throughout church life a realization must be fostered that solutions are usually easier to implement when a difficulty is first recognized.

Sometimes the best way to deal with a problem is to wait for the right moment. Delay for a well-defined purpose is not denial; instead, it is a decision to act at the appropriate time. Emmet Fox, the Quaker from another generation, described a creative way of deciding to wait for the right time to act: "To leave a thing in God's hands does not mean simply to hand it over to God, and then forget all about it . . . it means that every time the subject comes to mind you affirm that God is solving the problem in His own good way, and that all will be well."[1] Putting things in God's hand, as Fox suggests, is a spiritual, creative, and productive way to deal with some problems—a process much different than foot-dragging or denial.

Your pastor needs you and other lay leaders to sort and solve problems, difficulties, and petty quarrels. Every church has at least one suppressed, toxic problem that needs to be honestly faced and healed. Often perpetual, debilitating problems lie buried under layers of stagnation, denial, or control that center around dominate personalities.

Here are ways to start the healing. View yourself and others in your church's leadership pool as being linked creatively to God when it seems impossible to fully examine an issue. Take courage. Communicate love. Then, set out to solve every problem that has obvious answers; much to your surprise, in the process guidance will often come for facing other problems that appear to be insurmountable.

In this problem-solving process, keep reminding yourself that you are a fellow laborer with the pastor and other lay leaders. But you are also in active partnership with the living Christ, who promises to guide and empower you. Those who want to sit next to Him at the heavenly banquet must be willing to clean out dusty attics or shine light in dark cellars in contemporary churches, where problems so often hide from public view.

Seeking and setting in motion God's remedy keeps the church robust, while at the same time making your pastor realize and rejoice that your congregation is doing significant work in your corner of the world.

Myth #2—My Opinion Is Truth

"I'm usually right."

Stating an opinion, when done with forceful words or a stubborn spirit, makes it difficult to use your reverse gear. It also makes it difficult for persons who mostly agree with you to suggest alternatives. Thus, in decision-making groups, persons with the most rigid opinions often feel alone or ignored; sometimes they do not understand why. The problem is that others do not know how to respond, so they don't.

Remember when you state your viewpoint that it is an opinion— nothing more or less—and you should label it as such. If others want to suggest your ideas should carry special weight because of your wisdom, piety, and/or experience, let them do so while you keep humble. But if you insist upon stating your opinions in an ultimate, inflexible manner, others will not listen seriously to you.

Let's face it—God's truth is bigger than any of us can imagine. Nothing the human mind thinks or the human voice says can fully explain the ways God works in the church and in the world. Thus, there is room for many opinions as we seek the Father's guidance.

But here is how this dilemma causes misunderstandings in decision-making groups. A pastor feels as if she is on an emotional hot seat when a lay leader acts as if he speaks for God. It is a difficult position. If the minister questions the opinion, she appears to be questioning God. Conversely, if she agrees with the stated opinion on its merit, others think they are being denied their right to speak rationally about the issue—and in a way, they are.

Without realizing it, those who believe their opinions are inerrant often try to control by saying, "God told me" or "I'm surprised that you have followed Christ so long and still think that way!" or "Christians have always believed this" or, "It's a proven fact that . . ." Fair-minded listeners always enjoy a bit of mischievous glee when another member of the group replies, "Oh, really?" or, "What makes you believe that?"

All who do kingdom work in groups, lay and clergy alike, might consider using this story to help judge their presuppositions and opinions. A certain witness in a courtroom was about to be sworn in with the traditional oath, "Do you swear to tell the truth, the whole truth, and nothing but the truth, so help you God?" The man replied, "Sir, if I told the truth, the whole truth and nothing but the truth, I would *be* God."[2] Let's rest the case—No lay leader ever speaks the whole truth for God.

Strengthen your influence and acceptance as a lay leader by making a clear distinction in your speech between opinion and fact. Facts are backed with data, validating evidence, and reliable sources. Opinions are feelings or judgments, often of the moment, that can be biased, slanted, or even uninformed. The Canadian poet Sir William Drummond, who lived near the turn of the twentieth century, offers incredible insight for speech in church decision groups. He said, "He who will not reason is a bigot; he who cannot reason is a fool; and he who does not reason is a slave."[3]

Let's be fair-minded. Most of us, without realizing it, have inflated opinions or biased conclusions about many issues. What we don't like or understand, we often assume won't work or isn't useful. This dynamic shows up in our reactions to music styles in worship, service schedules, color choices in a remodeling project, and even notions about how the church treats new people.

Of course, a conscientious pastor will likely want to know what you think about many issues, but he also needs you to allow others to form and state their opinions. And he also needs your energetic support of another's judgments just as you would support your own. Be careful not to put your pastor in an administrative box so he feels he is hostage to your opinion. Most pastors love working with people who know how to think accurately, while allowing others to have their own opinions and to evaluate the issues differently from the way they do.

Wait patiently. Worthy opinions are generally implemented, but it sometimes takes months or years. In 1690, the philosopher John Locke observed correctly, "New opinions are always suspect, and usually opposed, without any other reason but because they are not already common."[4] Share your ideas quietly and allow the sun and the rain to nourish them.

Myth #3—Somone Must Be Blamed
"Who caused this problem?"

Blaming and shaming create many problems in a church, sometimes placing a millstone around a church's heart. Blame sometimes mesmerizes a church so it cannot think of anything else so it never becomes what God intended it to be. The issue in refusing to play the blame game is for individuals to accept responsibility for their conduct, to own what is rightfully theirs, and then show the same mercy and sensitivity to others they hope others will show them. As a wise, old man from Appalachia observed, "Why is it that the one who always accuses others is the one who always excuses himself?"

Today's blame can cause far-reaching consequences that a church cannot overcome for a long time. About forty years ago, a vocal minority in a church near where we live blamed a staff member for making a $5,000 mistake. They called it stealing and insisted on taking it to civil court. The judge threw the matter out of court, calling it a mischief suit. That judgment should have ended the matter, but it didn't. Blaming became the order of the day, mostly because of the embarrassment the civil suit caused in the community. Soon a vocal minority pulled out to plant a new church. Those who stayed with the original church, as might be expected, were forced to prune existing ministries because of decreased income. The accused staff member was branded for life: his ministry never blossomed, and he lived his whole life under a cloud of unwarranted suspicion. And though most people have forgotten the issues a long time ago, petty problems still fester that can be traced to the blaming and shaming of more than four decades ago. To this day, the new church started by dissenters has a contentious congregational personality that causes an unhealthy environment for members and anyone who visits. Over the years, many who blamed the most in the past moved on because they could not stand the kind of church they helped create.

Here's the Christ-exalting remedy for dealing with blame. When something goes wrong in your church, fix it. Look past the blame to initiate corrective action. The problem with blaming, like many negative emotions, is that it costs too much.

Refusing to blame promotes peace and allows room for errors that come from risk-taking. Refusing to blame gives others the benefit of the doubt and makes forgiveness possible. Refusing to blame forces us to look for solutions. Refusing to blame helps us focus on corrections rather than on finding a culprit.

A serendipity sometimes flows to those who refuse to blame. They build up emotional and spiritual capital, so others are not so apt to blame them when they do something silly, ridiculous, or disastrous. I love the non-blaming acceptance of the old father in the biblical story of the Prodigal Son. He had no time to blame because he celebrated what mattered so much more than blame.

Myth #4—Conflict Must Be Avoided at Any Cost
"Let's keep peace at any price."

Since the church is the only organization in the world committed to lovingly accepting everyone, we should expect even more conflict than we have. Even the disciples argued about greatness while in the presence of Jesus (Mark 9:34). It seems some of them apparently enjoyed conflict or even causing it.

The church that seeks to avoid conflict at any cost should not expect to get much done for the kingdom. No group of individuals will ever totally agree on every detail. Someone must give in. The only way to avoid conflict completely is for everyone to live and work alone—an impossibility because by her essence, the church requires us to serve together. But many of the problems we expect to hurt the church, resulting from disagreements, never happen. We worry needlessly. U.S. President Calvin Coolidge's advice applies: "Never go out to meet trouble. If you will just sit still, nine cases out of ten someone will intercept it before it reaches you."[5]

Thus, it is necessary for lay leaders to increase their sense of charity and acceptance by remembering that most churches, in the name of Christian love, put up with absurdities from lots of people, including us.

In any group organized around democratic principles, there will be many viewpoints. For example, a five-person committee in one church consisted of a policeman, an insurance agency owner, a factory worker, a mechanic, and a truck driver. Think of the richness, however, they needed acceptance and patience in order to make decisions. Various perspectives can lead to good decisions, provided committee members do not maim each other in the process.

Conflict in the church, then, must be viewed as an inescapable fact of life. The issue is to manage conflict so it is creative, useful, and not destructive. In the church, this means allowing, or even expecting and encouraging, people to speak their convictions and share their best thoughts on a subject. There is always a place for people to stand up for what they believe, providing it is done in humility and with respect for others.

Your pastor is often disheartened when people do not speak their minds in a meeting. He is frustrated by those who must have their own way at any cost. And he is grievously disappointed by those who speak freely outside formal meetings but are silent inside the meeting. You can aid the progress of your church by leading an effort to accept the fact that conflict is real and that it can be useful.

At the same time, try to model ways of keeping focused on issues rather than allowing or causing subtle attacks on persons with differing views. Become a peacekeeping partner with your pastor by insisting that disagreements be seasoned with gentleness, affirmation, acceptance, and grace. And refuse to get huffy, have your feelings hurt, or withdraw emotionally from the group.

Myth #5—Nitpickers and Perfectionist Should Not Be Offended
"Have you heard about this problem?"

Two self-appointed critics who called themselves informants made an appointment to meet the minister on Monday morning. After sharing normal pleasantries, they announced their intention to share their not-so-inspiring findings. Here's the essence of their long conversation: "Now, Pastor, we wanted you to know we appreciate you and your wife. We think you're doing a great job, but we thought you would like to know what people are saying—things you will probably want to improve. Mrs. Recreational Talker says you are spending too much time with new people. Mrs. I.M. Whiner says you no longer thank God for new babies in your pastoral prayer. Mr. Fussy says the shut-ins are complaining because you are not giving them enough attention. Miss Particular says you don't mingle with people after the worship service. And we wonder, Pastor, if our church is friendly enough." These two good informants did not intend to kill the pastor, but they nearly nibbled him to death. They demonstrated the old quip, "A perfectionist is one whose pursuit of perfection often leads him to make a perfect nuisance of himself."[6]

Though most pastors might desire to be informed about lacks or oversights that really matter, every church has nitpickers who are unsatisfied with a pastor's priorities or performance. A chief source of pain for a pastor is the regret she feels when someone in a congregation expects more than she is able to give. And this anguish especially cuts to the heart when a pastor is deeply involved in ministries that can't be discussed, such as providing pastoral care to a couple determined to divorce, offering support to a family whose daughter is pregnant out of wedlock, ministering to a family whose son is dying of AIDS, which he contracted while attending a church college, or spending time with the finance committee chairman to figure out how to cope with a deficit caused when five giving families were transferred out of town with their jobs.

Church pillars can protect pastors from nitpickers by helping the pastor keep ministry issues in realistic perspective and by gently helping nitpickers see the bigger picture. You might try discussing the following principles in personal conversation with your pastor and in appropriate committees:

• *Evaluate.* Since all criticism is not accurate, it must be sorted out.

• *Ignore.* Some criticism comes from recreational talkers who mean no harm and expect no changes.

• *Seek discernment.* In personal spiritual development, pastors and lay leaders should seek guidance to distinguish the important from the trivial. Some of the most effective pastors have a kind of inner guidance system that helps them know who needs them the most and when.

• *Protect.* Lay leaders should protect the pastor from unreasonable criticism. This can be achieved by having an active and loving pastoral relations committee that serves as a screening group to evaluate any complaints about the pastor or to discuss concerns raised by the pastor. Care must be taken in establishing such a committee to be sure it is committed to advocacy rather than becoming adversarial.

• *Volunteer.* Legitimate concerns can be delegated to lay leaders. This becomes significantly easier for a pastor to do when a church pillar voluntarily steps forward to say, "I want to help you with this ministry."

• *Laugh.* While everyone deserves a fair hearing, sometimes pastors and lay leaders have to learn to laugh at the humor to be seen in ridiculous demands and comical situations.

Keep this central reality in mind—your minister is no super-pastor. He can't solve every problem and can't be everywhere at the same time. Nor should he be expected to. He is not flawless. The best he can give and the best anyone should expect is that he will do his reasonable best, and that should be good enough. It certainly is good enough from God's perspective.

Myth #6—What Has Been Must Always Be

"We've always done it that way."

Church history teaches interesting lessons about spiritual renewal and new beginnings. In every century, or perhaps in every generation, a reform or revival segment of the church springs up as a reaction against empty forms and lifeless traditions. These renewal efforts start out with the purpose of taking a renewed essence of the Christian faith to the cutting edge of its times. Then in a few years, the new group does an interesting and predictable thing: in almost hilarious ways, generally within twenty-five and certainly within seventy-five years, the new group finds itself preserving, defending, and propagating its traditions. It tends to out-traditionalize previous generations who headed the organizations they earlier abandoned.

Evidently, preserving traditions is an inevitable part of forming or perpetuating any group, denomination, or local church. Some wag remarked accurately, "In the church, we make a tradition out of anything we have done three or more times." It happens at all levels of church life—local, national, and international. Routines and practices tend to continue after the rationale on which a tradition was built is long forgotten.

Let's gladly admit the Christian faith has some traditions we never want to lose, such as singing hymns, preaching the Word, receiving the sacraments, and fellowship among believers. These rich traditions serve as channels of blessing and inspiration for us. Traditions that have not lost their meaning should be preserved and renewed.

But other traditions are not at all sacred—for example, when we have the Christmas program, where fellowship activities are held, where the pastor lives, who plays the organ, when services are held, what is our style of worship, who counts the offerings, who goes Christmas caroling, and what the pastor's spouse does in the church. One country church has a long-established tradition that the oldest male member serves as head usher. What a sad show-and-tell of tradition continues as the congregation sees this pitiful, arthritic man trying to do his duty.

Defense of traditions sounds something like this: "That's the way we always do it." "They won't like it if you change it." "Nobody seems to know why we do it that way." Why doesn't someone think to ask, "Who are *they?*"

Let's accept the facts—the winds of change are blowing everywhere. Change is more rapid now than ever before. Our forefathers in the faith often had generations to adjust to change, but we often have only a few weeks or months to adjust. The tornadic winds are all around us, the gale is blowing at top speeds, and the storm is not likely to slow down much in our lifetime. There is no need to fear, however, because God designed the church for facing storms, performing rescue efforts, and making safe landings. Therefore, church pillars must use the winds of change for rescuing the perishing and sailing to longed-for destinations. The alternative is to sit in the harbor waiting for the calm, which may never come. Traditions are good to celebrate but deadly to worship.

Every pastor needs an opportunity to institute in each church he serves unique ways of doing ministry. Sometimes that means some traditions will be changed, recrafted, or dropped. As a church pillar, take responsibility for being a go-between with an innovative pastor and the defenders of traditions. Try explaining prevailing traditions to a new pastor and encourage him to make changes gradually, meaningfully, and with full explanation to all affected persons. At the same time, when your pastor suggests new programs and procedures, champion the cause, promote the possibilities, run interference to dominate persons, and become his advocate to appropriate decision groups.

Though a "change for change's sake" mentality accomplishes very little, most churches will never increase their effectiveness without changing in some way on a fairly frequent basis. More churches are dying for change than are dying because of change. Though business writer John Cowan probably did not have church in mind, his advice is useful for us: "Get your ambitions down to size. . . . Don't think five years ahead; nothing will be the same then. . . . Usually all the distracting noises in an organization in flux turn out to be just noises. Focus on what you are trying to do. Do it."[7]

Try to keep a long view. Keep in mind, today's revolutionary ideas will probably be tomorrow's staid traditions. After much debate, one church I served instituted the revolutionary idea of having a Living Lord's Supper at Easter. How the saints resisted with a thousand questions about precedent, cost, church dramatics, and grown men walking barefooted in church. Now, thirty years later, the same church advertises this service as a thirty-year tradition and looks at the event as something they would not want to be without. In my heart, I wonder if the ritual has lost its meaning, but I pity any pastor who tries to change it. Traditions are like that. It tries a pastor's spirit and undercuts his imagination if at least some lay leaders are not ready to help abandon worn-out traditions and begin new ones.

Disagreements over methodologies create havoc in the church. Churches divide over methods more than over doctrinal disagreements. Meanwhile, we must face the fact that many of yesterday's methods are meaningless, especially for pastors and parishioners who grew up in this newer generation. None of us or our forebearers have ever played in this new arena before. Resemblances to the past are purely coincidental. The "tried and true" has been tried but it is not necessarily true. James Bell reminds us, "No matter our task, we must search for new and better methods—for even that which we now do well must be done better tomorrow."[8] To survive, the church must learn to accept, embrace, and even use the unexpected to her advantage.

Wise is the lay leader who promotes and practices the principle that more than one method may be used to achieve the same goal. The principle is this—agree on our objective and then try whatever method seems most effective. Try giving those who originate an idea as much liberty as possible in developing a methodology; otherwise, they will feel frustrated by methods they do not embrace.

Myth #7—My Excuses Are Valid

"I didn't realize what was expected."

You have probably heard most of the excuses: "I didn't know what was expected." "I didn't have enough time." "My committee let me down." "It took more time than I thought." "I was afraid to take too much authority." "I was surprised at the expense, so I thought you might want to reconsider." Perhaps you have even given these excuses yourself.

Excuses are a way we let ourselves off for placing the church work in low priority. When someone else misses a deadline, we consider it a lack of priority or even incompetence. But when we miss a deadline, we rationalize that we have a valid reason.

Excuses and rationalizations about the Christian leader's time commitments melt like ice cream in the sun when we hear the reality check suggested by Vance Havner: "While we are puttering, life gets away. . . .we are so busy with the here and now that we forget the eternal. If you are too busy to find time for God, you are too busy. You have received a charge to keep, and if your busyness keeps you from being about your Father's business, you are a poor businessman."[9] Ouch!

One of the most frustrating experiences a pastor faces is the exceedingly slow pace of deciding, acting, and achieving in the church. The issue frustrates the pastor even more when the work of the church is compared with the way we get things done in our personal lives and in our occupations—personal stuff generally goes faster than church commitments. While a faithful pastor would not want to deny the necessity for accomplishments in anyone's personal and vocational life, he needs lay leaders to place the church in higher priority. And one can't really excuse rationalization by saying, "I'm only a volunteer" when we remember who it is we volunteered to serve.

Myth #8—My Experience Works in Every Situation
"This is the way it worked in our other church."

No church is like it once was or like the one of our childhood. Like a sleepy creek in the country that looks as it did in bygone years, the church constantly changes in subtle, almost imperceptible ways. But it changes continuously.

That reality is hard to accept. When we hear the word *church,* most of us do not think about what the Bible says, what the ancient creeds declare, or what theology explains. Instead, we usually think of the little church in the wildwood where we grew up, or the beautiful edifice on Main Street in the town where we attended high school, or the storefront chapel in an urban neighborhood where we were introduced to the Gospel. Church—the grand, old word and the warm family feeling from our past—creates as many mental images as there are persons to think them. Our memories are a lot like the old man who reminisced, "My baseball batting skills keep getting better as I grow older." Our ideas about church and its meaning in our past grow more tender, more nostalgic, but less accurate with passing years. So we idealize the past and wish we could recreate a church like the one we think we remember.

One church member who would like to be a lay leader in his church is never elected to a responsible post because he universalizes

84

his past church experiences. He wants his pastor in one of America's largest cities to duplicate the ministry he remembers from rural Iowa, where the pastor called in his parents' home at least once a month and preached on Sundays—that was the extent of most of his pastoral efforts. But consider the incredibly different demands. A pastor who serves in his city now has to take up to three hours in heavy traffic to make calls in various hospitals. To complicate matters, ill people are sometimes admitted to hospitals fifty miles away at a regional medical center. It is simply impossible for a contemporary pastor to duplicate the way things used to be in a different time and in a different place.

What is gone is gone, but we must find ways to make this day great for ministry. Thus, rather than grieving over our loss, pastors and lay leaders must recapture the impact the church made in former days in some new way today and tomorrow. The issue is not technique, tradition, or past ritual but impact, influence, and Christ-exalting relationships.

To help a pastor keep a church focused on ministry in the present, church pillars must avoid universalizing their church experiences from the past. They must encourage themselves and others to focus on today. The answer seems clear but hard to do—lead your church to live in the present moment in an exciting relationship with Christ and satisfying associations with each other. Then turn down the TV and stereo, clatter and gossip, and listen carefully to how the Spirit wants your church to impact this generation.

As a church leader, you can work to make fellow believers aware of the challenges the church faces in contemporary society. Show them how many ways you are trying to make your pastor great and how you are meeting the challenges of living a Christlike existence yourself. Your determination will inspire others and help them see how happy, meaningful relationships with your spiritual leader enrich everyone in the fellowship and help the church focus its ministry on present opportunities and contemporary issues.

Myth #9—Our Pastor Should Do Better
"I wish we had a stronger leader."

Pastor Stefan Smith had faults that his church members easily recognized, sometimes discussed among themselves, and even made some wish he would move. But Stefan also had strengths. He cared for his congregation and showed it. He preached well, so his sermons were thoughtful, occasionally confrontational, and always biblical. Some considered him distant, but he was actually shy. Some thought he was too studious, though he was really serious about understanding the meaning of Scripture and applying it to life. Some thought his marriage and children had too high a place in his priorities; he was actually committed to avoiding problems in his family that his "absentee father" created in his childhood. In fact, Stefan's commitments to his family were a beautiful model of Christian marriage and parenting for the young families in the church. In order to be sacrificial with his stewardship, he was as frugal as possible in his lifestyle, and his family lived as simply as possible. Some church members struggled to understand and accept his priorities.

Finally, after five years of service to his first church, Stefan accepted a call to another church in a town fifty miles away. He was too gracious to tell anyone the real reasons for leaving, but he wrote in his journal, "I am tired of criticism, so I think it is time to move to a new assignment."

Three months after Pastor Smith left, the church realized what they had lost. Some wondered aloud what they could have done to keep him from leaving. They were right to ask whether the situation could have been remedied with a bit more affirmation, a raise in salary, a new attic fan in the parsonage, or a book allowance of $500 per year.

Sometimes no one thinks about how things look or feel to a pastor. A dedicated young pastor, with three growing children, sacrificed for six years to plant a church; now the church is doing well and recently moved into a new building—largely through the leadership efforts of its pastor. Someone thought it would be a good idea to show the congregation's appreciation to the pastor by giving him a $10 per week raise. No one in the decision group apparently understood how long his family had been scraping along financially. The pastor appreciated the raise, and he told the decision group so. But his family needed a minimum of four times that amount. Due to six years of low salary, this pastor was forced by economic necessity to move to another assignment. Sadly, the church could have paid more, but they were afraid "to create unrealistic expectations for future raises." Ironically, the moving bill for the new pastor was $5,000, and they increased his salary $35 per week.

Maybe it is risky business to ask why pastors leave. Or maybe it is the exact thing to ask. Like one laywoman said to me, "I once asked a pastor why he was leaving and he told me. I learned more about a pastor's financial problems than I wanted to know. I will never ask a pastor that question again because it might make us grieve over what we could have done to change things."

Though you might think her reaction a bit unusual, perhaps every church decision group would do itself a great favor by regularly affirming the pastor's strengths—accentuate the positive, as the old song says. Maybe it is best done on a personal basis, but it must be done. Why not consider yourself a one-member committee to start a campaign of random acts of kindness to your pastor and his family?

Celebrate his character, commitments, and competencies. Honor his passionate sense of mission and his nurturing efforts for the people in your parish. In such an atmosphere of accepting affirmation, many pastors will stretch to be as good as people think they are.

A laywoman whom he had not seen for twenty years opened her heart to her former pastor. "If only we had known what a treasure we had when you were our pastor, we would have done anything to keep you," she said. "More money, appreciation, understanding—more anything—it seems like a small price when it is compared to the confusion we had for ten years after you left."

Your pastor is a priceless treasure God has given your church. Cherish his ministry and try to recognize his full value to the life of your church and in the destiny of your soul.

Myth #10—Confusing Carelessness and Faithfulness

"The pastor is the reason they left the church."

We've all heard it sometime: "You mean the Newmans are leaving the church? It can't be; he's been a lay leader for years. I hear the Thompsons are thinking about joining another church too. Where are they going and why? The Newmans were raised in this church. It's like losing a member of our family. They say they are not being fed from the pulpit!"

Since we live in a consumer society, it is easy to move to another fellowship for shallow or even selfish reasons. But it's a kick in the stomach and a stab in the heart when a pastor hears, usually by way of the grapevine, that someone is leaving to attend a church where the people are "friendly" and the preacher is "sensational."

Of course, in these matters kindness, charity, and tenderness always must be shown by all parties and to all parties. There may be biblical reasons for leaving a church, like apostate preaching, impure practices, or gross incompetence. But even those issues need correction with the spirit of Jesus.

A departing member owes it to his spiritual well-being to be sure he is not asking, "What can I get out of the church?" rather than, "What can I do for Christ through the church?" When situations get complicated and snarled, a pastor is sometimes blamed for carelessness when the real problem may be created by his faithfulness. Some people leave because of the demands of discipline, or their unwillingness to be faithful stewards. Some leave because of accurate biblical preaching that requires what Scripture demands or because of alluring attractions of the world. If the pastor's careful and loving proclamation of the Word of God is the problem, their leaving should be seen as a healthy symptom of a pastor's faithfulness to his call.

The migration of members is a pressing problem that requires much more thought than this book allows. The issue highlighted here is that every member departure cannot be blamed on a pastor's neglect. Some responsibility has to be borne by the departing member or by the congregation.

Many pastors have left the ministry permanently because they could not deal with the feelings of failure over losing people they loved. Many suffer grief and a sense of loss. They cannot bring themselves to explain the real issues to those who remain. They feel rejected by those they served in times of crisis—almost abandoned and betrayed. Some blame themselves and some even think they goofed in dealing with eternal issues. They are just not able to shake the idea that they failed; they are called by God to serve people, and the apparent failure hurts.

Lay leaders can help diffuse this situation by doing the following:

1. Don't panic—God is still in control.
2. Examine yourself and your church's ministry for flaws and blemishes.
3. Correct the flaws and blemishes.
4. Make sure those who leave know they can come back, provided they have not been destructive in the process of leaving.
5. Show kindness to all parties as you downplay gossip and curiosity.
6. Accept the reality that not everyone will be happy in every church.
7. Cultivate a spirit of serving the church rather than a spirit of taking from the church. Meaningful service is where most of us find our greatest fulfillment.
8. Recognize it's almost impossible to help church hoppers who expect a church to cater to their whims.
9. Move ahead in victory.

Solving These Myths in Your Church

If we could have continued listening in on the discussion between Pastor Adams and Pastor McWilliams at the beginning of this chapter, the list of dilemmas would have grown. Every pastor has his own list. Every congregation probably has a list too. Since the lists vary so much according to pastor and church, how can hidden-agendas and conversational taboos be discussed, understood, and solved?

First, we have to get past what one minister said of his first three years of ministry in a particular church: "The first year, they idolized me; the second year, they tantalized me; and the third year, they scandalized me." Each stage of development and relationship has built-in difficulties that need to be discussed, understood, and solved.

Work to improve communication between your pastor, yourself, and other church pillars. Some communication strategies can be structured, and scheduled once every three months. Other conversations can be informal, such as lunch or dinner with the pastor and a small group of lay leaders. Dialogue, affirmation, and understanding are the goals. Not every lay leader, not every pastor, not every church will be comfortable with these methods, but efforts to improve communication need to be implemented. The inaction at first may be awkward, but most worthwhile conversations start that way. Initiate and design the process in whatever way you feel comfortable, but do it.

These following discussion stimulators between leaders and pastors will start a flow of ideas—no more than one or two in each session, please:

1. How close is our church to fulfilling its mission?
2. What expectations do you have that are not being fulfilled?
3. What can we do to make your ministry more effective? Is it a new desk, a new computer, or even increased secretarial help?
4. What is the most affirming word or act you have ever received from a lay leader in any church?
5. What do you do in the church that a lay person could do as well? Or, what do you do in the church that I could do to help you?
6. Does your spouse and family feel cherished in our church? If yes, how? If no, why not?
7. What changes need to be made in our church to encourage you to remain as our pastor for the next fifteen years?
8. What core values are we unintentionally overlooking?
9. If you had five uncommitted days with which to do anything you wanted, what would you do?
10. How would you adjust the present priorities in our church?

Laity always want sensitive, competent pastors, just as they should. At the same time, pastors pray for committed, gifted laity who are deeply devoted to Christ. Since there are not enough ideal pastors or ideal laity to go around, you have a magnificent opportunity to help each other grow into what God wants you both to become. A common belief is that a great pastor makes a great church, and it is often true. But the converse is also true—committed laity shape and mold pastors into greatness.

Overcoming the Myths

Author Laurie Jones offers a grand reason for looking beyond all the debilitating church myths: "Jesus wants leaders to constantly look for ways to expand their vision, their influence, and their contribution. There are always more possibilities than our eyes can see."[10] All these possibilities provide an extraordinary opportunity for everyone to grow.

RENEWAL STRATEGIES FOR CHURCH PILLARS
Helps for Unmasking the Myths

1. Denying problems often makes them multiply.

2. Insisting on your way undermines church unity.

3. Blaming exaggerates most problems.

4. Keeping peace at any price may be too expensive.

5. Pleasing nitpickers is impossible.

6. Worshiping the past seldom inspires renewal.

7. Testing your excuses against standards you use to judge another's rationalizations.

8. Recognizing that every church is different and every new generation in the same congregation is distinct.

9. Valuing your pastor's strengths helps you see past his weaknesses.

10. Defending your pastor's faithfulness, especially when it is being called carelessness.

honor the past
live in the present
plan for the future

"Church members have much more to do than go to church as curious, idle spectators, to be amused and entertained. It is their business to pray mightily that the Holy Spirit will clothe the preacher and make his words like dynamite."

Wilbur Chapman

5. THE SATISFACTION FACTOR

The Jesus Way of Counting Greatness

Father, send renewal so we cherish what You cherish. Give our leadership team—laity and clergy—delightful satisfaction in service. Help us view service assignments as a captivating honor given by You to us. Rid us of self-pity and low motivation. Give us a sense of the glory of Christian service. Amen.

"Who cleaned Noah's ark?" How foolish that question sounds until it forces you to face the most basic issue a church leader ever faces: Am I willing to genuinely serve? While we often seek position or social standing, Christ offers dirty hands, fatigued bodies, disillusioned dreams, deadly crosses, and slain egos.

Let me explain how the question "Who cleaned the ark?" started. It began while I (H.B.) watched a Focus on the Family video entitled *Noah and the Ark* with my grandson, Taylor. Beverly, my wife, and Taylor grew weary watching the story over and over. But the animated actions and biblical message intrigued me. The longer I watched, the more I felt captivated by the question "Who cleaned the ark?"

Somebody had to do it. Think of the problems poor Noah faced. All those animals in a crowded space for many months, the smell got worse with all those wet days outside and the dampness inside. It must have been a horrible task to clean the ark. Perhaps Noah finally said to those with him, "Well, guys, I'm tired of doing this cleaning by myself. It's your turn." Or maybe he found a volunteer who said, "Noah, I'll clean out the ark today. You don't have to worry about it. I'll do it. And I'll do it right."

Then I started asking myself, "Who cleans out arks now?" It's nearly impossible to get an accurate national picture of volunteerism. Many congregational leaders think volunteerism has dropped significantly, and others insist it is on its deathbed. Meanwhile, secular literature reports volunteerism is increasing in nonchurch organizations. The differences are difficult to sort through. Apathy, however, is a main topic whenever pastors get together. They want to know how to overcome creeping lethargy and epidemic passiveness. They ask out loud, "How can I motivate people to do what needs to be done?"

Dealing with Apathy

Since apathy seems so rampant in the church, all of us who claim the name of Christ must scrutinize our commitments and validate our motivations for what we do for Christ through His church.

The more significant self-examination questions are:
• What do we do for the kingdom of God?
• Why do we do what we do, when we do it?
• What is the result of the effort we invest in the church?
• If Jesus stood in physical form before us today, would He find us faithful?
• Would Christ find us challenged by kingdom needs?
• Would He find us willing, involved, and committed?
• Would He find us resolute for accomplishing His will?

Being a genuine servant of Christ means giving up all fascination with status and stature to follow Jesus. The One who drew followers with a basin and towel, a lethal cross, and a leave-everything summons, calls us to follow Him too.

Lots of believers have duped themselves about serving. They think they are doing better than they are. It's not too difficult to trick ourselves into believing serving means holding office and attending church. But every church has officeholders who give very little effective service. It's easy to confuse position with performance, or to think church status is actually serving Christ, or that prominence is authentic kingdom achievement. But it's not.

Let's stop fooling ourselves. Service, performance, and achievement for Christ mean we get our hands dirty, we get our clothing bloody, and we put our reputations on the line. Serving means we wipe away tears, cry with those who hurt, get involved in the lives of others, and feel a holy anger over the consequences sin produces in individuals and our world. It means we feed the hungry, clothe the naked, bind up the broken, and intercede for those who have lost their way.

Achievement for Christ means we speak up for truth and let everyone know whose side we are on. It means we clean arks, dig ditches, question our assumptions, love troubled teens, visit elderly shut-ins, practice childlike faith, and witness to what Christ is doing in us. It means we are never the same after we try something too big for us in the name of our Lord. In caring for others, we find our peace, satisfaction, and energy for being overcomers in the details of our lives. More and more we see that what we do for others in Jesus' name is as much for us as it is for those we serve or for God. Every act of service shapes us into Christlikeness in some way.

Christian service causes many confusing contradictions. Unbelievers are amazed. How can it be, they marvel, that serving in the name of Jesus creates more satisfaction for the people of God than all the high-sounding titles or prominent positions the world offers. Sadly, the church sometimes forgets this when it promotes servants to prominent positions, where they tend to forget the Lord's instructions: "The greatest among you will be your servant. For whoever exalts himself will be humbled, and whoever humbles himself will be exalted" (Matt. 23:11-12).

Lessons from the Serving Christ

To prevent such counterfeiting of genuine Christianity, our Lord warned His disciples (and us) just after He washed their feet, "I have set you an example that you should do as I have done for you. I tell you the truth, no servant is greater than his master, nor is a messenger greater than the one who sent him" (John 13:15-16).

Evidently, serving, suffering, and salvation are powerfully connected in our Lord's thinking, even as they are in our living and caring for others. He leaves very little room for titles, prominence, or status. According to our Lord's teaching here, our service is to be modeled after His, and He doesn't mention standing, position, or power. Then, to forever clinch this truth in the disciples' minds, Jesus adds a magnificent summary sentence, "If you understand what I'm telling you, act like it—and live a blessed life" (John 13:17).[1] This teaching is sobering for every church leader, layperson, and pastor.

Sometimes we seriously wonder if the greatest logjam in contemporary Christianity is the unwritten commitment to status, standing, and prominence—things that are so important to insiders and so pointless to outsiders.

Several lessons from this passage will save lots of difficulties in the work of the church and in the life of individual Christians. Let's consider them together.

Service Impacts All Relationships in the Kingdom

Listen closely to the teaching of Christ: we are to "wash each other's feet" (v. 14). True humility toward other believers keeps us realistic about service and realistic about ourselves. We are nobodies whom Christ has appointed to serve in His stead; that doesn't make us the Christ but humbly keeps us understanding who we really are—mere sinners saved by grace.

Though the passage teaches many things, one of its startling messages to leaders is that everyone needs to serve fully as much as everyone needs to be served. It teaches that when we put others first, then our needs are met in the process or they pale into insignificance.

A servant serves regardless of her rank, position, or status. What does a servant do? She serves. That means a servant looks at those about her to see what needs doing and volunteers to do it. Nothing gets done for Christ until someone takes a towel and basin and does something. That task may be as far below your station in life as foot washing was for the Master. In a word, servanthood is *self-sacrifice*—giving up your rights to your position, time, standing, and rank to fill a need in someone else's life.

The Satisfaction Factor

Sometimes lay pillars and pastors have the mistaken idea that the church owes them something because of their loyalty, faithfulness, or seniority. Not so. The Lord always keeps us in His debt by all of His wonderful provisions for us. Thus, our only reasonable response to His continuous generosity is to try giving in the same measure of devotion as He has given to us, realizing all the time such giving can never be accomplished in an ultimate sense.

The world is filled with takers, but the authentic church is filled with givers. That's one of the most significant differences between leaders in the church and leaders in the world. Outside the church, leaders are takers. Inside the church, Jesus expects leaders to be givers. And He expects that the intensity of our giving will be gauged by the pressing needs we see around us.

One of the most impressive ways service impacts relationships in the church can be seen in a story from a church H.B. served as pastor. A serving disciple in the congregation was a civil judge, a learned, scholarly man who looked every bit the part of his profession. But at church, one of the ways he chose to serve was to minister to three-year-old children. Every Sunday morning he came to church carrying a duffel bag that contained a jumpsuit. He would go into the restroom, put his jumpsuit on over his pinstriped suit, and then move to the three-year-olds' classroom, where he helped teach children.

At first, H.B. made a big deal of this man's service and said, "This is below you. You can better serve the church in another capacity. Please let me find something else for you to do. We can't have a judge doing such a menial task."

The judge responded, "Pastor, please let me do what I feel called to do. I love working with the children. I look forward to doing this each week."

Consider the incredible results that came from his service. The children loved him so much he was like a Pied Piper when he came into the church—they came from all over to greet him and to pull on his legs. Children who had outgrown the three-year-olds' class loved being around him too. Even though he served children, he also made a great impression on parents. Though the judge could have sought positions of great visibility and power, he knew who he was and what

God wanted him to do. In his serving, he touched lots of people: he loved children and they loved him back; he challenged others to find their place of service; and he helped his pastor see how serving impacts many different relationships in the church.

Service Challenges Status/Standing in the Church

The passage in John says, "no servant is greater than his master, nor is a messenger greater than the one who sent him" (v. 16). Try applying the teachings of this passage to the elitist terms we love to use, like "senior pastor," "key lay leader," "long-time board member," "lifelong missionary," "his holiness, the bishop," or even "the greatest Christian I have ever met."

Apparently some of the reasons Jesus took the towel was to teach lessons about giving up status and not taking one's position too seriously. No doubt as the disciples followed Jesus they loved the adulation and attention our Lord received from the crowds. Perhaps that made them desire some of the same attention. Watching Christ, the disciples could easily have concluded that following Him would give them status and a high position in the kingdom. Subsequent Scriptures show that was a big part of their thinking about their future in the kingdom.

But Jesus wanted the disciples to know that following Him would shape them. It always does. He showed them in unmistakable terms that they were to be servants. That was a message few leaders in other religious movements in history had been forced to learn. But they were. Jesus, seeing what was in the minds of the disciples, even as He knows what is in our minds, decided it was time to teach a hard lesson. As the Scripture says about our Lord, "Who, being in very nature God, did not consider equality with God something to be grasped, but made himself nothing, taking the very nature of a servant" (Phil. 2:6-7). That's exactly what He did in the Upper Room. He took on Himself the form of a servant to show us all that love is the driving force behind effective ministry.

The situation baffled the disciples. You remember that Jesus as a rabbi possessed the highest social and ecclesiastical credentials—one of the most distinguished positions of honor anyone could have in Israel.

Yet He lowered Himself to perform the task of a servant and washed their feet. By doing so He "showed them the full extent of His love" (John 13:1).

Service Supplies Satisfaction

Jesus told His disciples, "You will be blessed if you do [these things]" (v. 17). Even though servanthood seems out of sync with many secular values, it provides incredible satisfaction for servants. An inner-city mission minister, when asked about serving down-and-outers in his city, replied, "I'm sure I get more pure joy distributing clothing and food to the needy than the satisfaction all the brass get from running my denomination. I am blessed." Though his statement could use more charity, it is important for all church leaders to realize that serving is why Christ called us. And that is where adventure, fulfillment, and fun are.

Serving is one of the best opportunities to discover pure joy in the human journey. Helping another find his way helps us find the Way. God forbid that any leader ever gets to the place where he wants to be served more than to serve.

Service Is Sometimes Difficult to Receive

The passage in John records Peter saying, "No, You shall never wash my feet" (v. 8). Peter felt deeply troubled by the notion that Jesus would wash his feet. He, like many devoted followers of Christ, seemed more able to give service than to receive it—a common ailment even today.

There is something of Peter in many of us. Peter couldn't stand the humiliation of having his feet washed by his Master, so he refused Him.

Jesus answered, "Unless I wash you, you have no part with Me."

Peter replied, "Then, Lord, not just my feet but my hands and my head as well."

Everyone needs to learn this lesson. Real service is a two-way relationship that both blesses and humiliates those who give and receive service.

Service Is Sometimes Unspectacular

Foot-washing at the Passover feast was something that just had to be done. Nobody stood in line to assume the responsibility. It bore no honor. Nothing else could begin, however, until the disciples had their feet washed—like washing our hands before dinner in our culture. The meal could not be served until everyone had clean feet. The custom was usually done by a hired servant, but never by the host or guest of honor.

So many routine things need to be done to keep the church ready for ministry each week. So many people need help. So many would believe if somebody cared a little bit more. There are always more routine tasks that need doing.

Foot-washing was like that. It was not the main event of this meeting. In a similar way, our serving may not be the main event at church, but it contributes to the main event. No church could do its ministries for long without the routine, behind-the-scenes work of many devoted people.

Service Is Love in Action

Scripture teaches, "Let us not love with words or tongue but with actions and in truth" (1 John 3:18). James echoes the same idea: "Faith by itself, if it is not accompanied by action, is dead. . . . faith without deeds is useless" (James 2:17, 20). Sounds as if John and James were writing to us.

Much talk and little action fill our world. Some church committees talk for years about doing something, but nothing happens except more talk. To talk about something is not to do anything. Few things are ever done until they are thoroughly discussed, but many thoroughly discussed things are never done.

So often servants of Christ feel stymied by not knowing exactly what to do or by not being able to do sensational service. We look at great persons of influential faith like Mother Teresa, Billy Graham, and Charles Colson but can't image we could ever live up to their levels of serving. The good news is you are not expected to do what they do. We are obligated to do what we can—that's all, but that's a lot.

We tend to think servanthood means giving enormous sums of

money, doing monumental deeds, or dying sacrificially for a great cause. The foot-washing event, however, demonstrates that service is doing simple, non-spectacular things just because they need to be done. It is doing the ordinary with the most uncommon motivation.

Much of the time, serving includes elementary things like giving a hungry man a meal, a thirsty woman a drink, a sick person a prayer, a prisoner a word of hope, a widow a helping hand, or a confused child a chunk of time. In short, service is developing a heart for doing what Jesus would do in the setting where you have been providentially placed. It is asking yourself continuously, "What needs to be done that God wants me to do?"

Jesus clarified the service question by simply saying, "I tell you the truth, whatever you did not do for one of the least of these, you did not do for Me" (Matt. 25:45). His list of service included helping the hungry, thirsty, naked, sick, and imprisoned.

There is an important lesson here. Apparently, all effective Christian service starts with small things that are not too difficult: a phone call saying, "I missed you Sunday"; a note in the mail saying, "I saw a report of your accomplishment in the newspaper—congratulations." It's telling at least one person every day you are thinking and praying for him or her. Do it in person, write a note, or make a phone call.

Some churches have changed their whole atmosphere by starting an encouragement card strategy like H.B. had at his Pasadena and Salem churches. Encouragement cards are placed in the pew racks so people can write a word of thanks or encouragement to someone and then drop the card in the offering plate. The church office then addresses the card and mails it. One encouragement card often makes a great positive impact.

For most of us, the meaning of service is wrapped up in little things that bring joy to the life of others. Think of the list of small things people remember: "He mowed my yard when I was sick." "She cared for my child while I went to the hospital." "He sent me flowers when I needed them most." "She called with an encouraging word." "He told me I could never get away from Jesus no matter how hard I tried."

Try majoring on lonely people. For some reason, people seem to have either too much togetherness or too much loneliness—they are seldom in balance. Though these extremes are difficult to control, loneliness and people weariness come to us all. Regrettably, when we are most saturated with people may be the exact time when others are suffering from loneliness. The lonely people are usually the ones who have recently lost loved ones or who have experienced severe changes in their jobs, health, or locations. Some have outlived friends. In their eighties and nineties, many spend lots of time going to funerals of family and friends, and many spend even more time thinking of their own parting. Some feel lonely in crowds. This happened to Neil when he spoke at a wonderful pastors' group where he did not know one person. And loneliness almost overwhelmed me (H.B.) when I put my last child and grandchild on the plane following a wonderful family Christmas.

For purposes of serving others in the name of our Lord, it is wise to remember that everyone we meet has some grief, some loneliness, some separation, and some hurt they feel but are not ready to discuss. There is a place in our service for God where we develop sensitivities to these issues and offer people support even when we do not know the extent of their difficulties.

Value of Service Is Not Determined by Response

The value of service rendered in Jesus' name can never be determined by the response of those who receive the service. Disciples at the footwashing had little understanding of what Jesus was doing or what His words meant. Those we serve are sometimes oblivious too. The other day a motorist stopped his car on a busy street to take a toddler out of the street and back to the child's mother. The mother was preoccupied, had not missed the child, and was in no frame of mind to thank the motorist who saved her child from almost certain death. However, those of us who watched greatly appreciated what the motorist did. Christian service is like that—it may take years or eternity for us and others to see the real issues.

Since the service Jesus provided often had a delayed response in people, we should not be surprised if that happens to us. We all have done things and then waited for a thank-you note that never came. We have done things that seemed unimportant at the time to those who received them and the enemy said, "See, you put yourself out to serve and sacrifice for others. But they didn't even notice, or if they noticed, they didn't even care."

An important kingdom service principle to remember is that we serve to please the Lord. He has to be pleased, and we generally know if we are pleasing to Him. If others appreciate us, we can take that as a serendipity; however, we do not serve for the praise of people but for the development of godliness. Our goal is to become more like Christ. In its finest hour, service is giving in the name of Jesus without counting the cost or hungering for praise or credit.

Service Must Be Done with Joy

The psalmist loved to sing, "Shout for joy to the Lord, all the earth. Serve the Lord with gladness; come before Him with joyful songs" (Ps. 100:1-2). As I hear in my mind the psalmist sing, I think of thousands of sour-faced, dull people who serve Jesus because they are afraid not to do so. Sadly, they miss the fun of service by always thinking of it as a "duty I have to do." Their idea is, "I will do my duty no matter how much I hate the work." Such an attitude creates its own problem. Who wants a personal evangelist who hates evangelism? Or a youth minister who dislikes teenagers? Or a lay leader who would rather be at the lake on Sunday than in the house of God? The casual prospect for the church had the right question in mind when he asked the people at his door, "Did you come to my house because you wanted to come or because you were sent?" Being sent is better than not going. But there is a special joy beyond duty that energizes Christian service.

Let's refocus this point. As servants, we have many reasons to sing, and shout, and laugh. Psalm 100 explains we can sing in our service because we know the Lord is God (3); He has made us and we are His (3); His love endures forever (5); and His faithfulness continues across all generations (5). Try putting that list before you when you start to think Christian service is a dreary duty or a demeaning assignment.

Sing, laugh, shout, and skip your way into meaningful service. No one can effectively serve in Jesus' name without His nearness and His enablement. Serve Christ and His people with joy—it's the only way to go. The writer of Hebrews offers wonderful advice about service: "Let us consider how we may spur one another on toward love and good deeds" (Heb. 10:24). People respond more quickly and more positively to those who serve Christ with joy.

Servanthood Makes Christians Grow

It is doubtful that an idle Christian ever grows very much spiritually. The old argument that we must be something before we can do something is like the "chicken or egg" debate. No doubt being helps our doing, but sometimes doing something for another person changes our being forever. Visiting an AIDS ward provides an entirely new perspective for most Christians. Offering a year of volunteer service to a third-world country changes most people. Our friend Dr. Gary Morsch, a physician and gatherer of medical supplies for poor nations, is often lauded for his efforts, but he is the first to tell you he is becoming more like Christ in the effort. That's a pretty significant serendipity, isn't it? One writer remarked, "Give yourself to a great cause. You may not do the cause much good, but the cause will do you a lot of good."

Let's remember service opportunities are to help us accomplish something important for God and to aid our fellow humans. But the seldom-discussed benefit is what service does for the servant.

Four lines of poetry from an old clipping file say it well:

> All the blessings the Lord is bestowing
> > Just pass them along as you may:
> For 'tis true of the things of the Spirit,
> > We but keep what we've given away.

But you ask, "How can I use Christian service opportunities to help me grow? How can I transform opportunities for helping others to make me more like Christ? How does this two-way idea work in practical, everyday acts of service? Do you really mean I become more like Christ as I serve His people?"

At the heart of these questions is our assumption that everyone wants to grow in effective service and Christlikeness. You likely would not have read this far if you did not agree with that assumption. Consequently, if you are ready to take a giant step of faith, you can pray these three simple petitions. Be careful—these prayers may change your life forever.

1. Lord, stretch my mind. Help me to understand how big the world is. Help me see how many live on the globe.

Once Dr. Jerry Falwell said to H.B., "London, you worry me. I don't think your vision is big enough."

H.B. argued with him, and Falwell replied, "What is your vision?"

H.B. answered, "To be one of the largest churches in Salem, Oregon."

Falwell countered, "You already are."

Then as the main point began to dawn on H.B., Dr. Falwell continued, "At Lynchburg, we believe Lynchburg is our city, Virginia our state, and America our parish."

Such a vision stretches anyone's mind. But consider what would happen if every lay leader reading this book would start to see the world as the responsibility of their church. Something spiritually revolutionary would take place in America that would change the course of history. Scores of people will find Christ when our vision is extended beyond what we expect and beyond what is ordinary, normal, or predictable. Ask God to stretch your mind, enlarge your vision, and destroy your limiting stereotypes.

2. Lord, sensitize my conscience. Make me angry with what makes You angry. Violence, killings, dope, decay of a soul, and the declining value on human life must sadden God's heart. He must weep over broken families where teenage girls have babies and teenage boys kill each other for sport. In this petition for a sensitized conscience, pray that God will help you see that a church fortress can never lead people to Christ. Ask God to soften your spirit so you can feel the pain, brokenness, cheating, and entrapments of people around you.

Ask God to sensitize your conscience to everything He wants changed. Pray for grace and grit to change what you can in your sphere of influence. Pray God will save you from cursing the darkness when you could light a candle or start a holy fire.

You ask, "How do I start?" There is no sure way. But to feel their pain you have to get close to hurting people. Try serving food in a mission, volunteer at a school for academically challenged kids, start a food pantry in your church, or give a few hours per month to a halfway house. Try going to an AA meeting or visiting an AIDS hospital ward. Seeing, feeling, and knowing create a holy unrest and gnawing dissatisfaction of superficial piety. It will take you outside your comfort zone so the church becomes more than a place to take in a service or two as time allows. When you pray for a sensitized conscience, you no longer settle for good things and nice programs.

3. Lord, strengthen my courage. Disturb me, anger me, disrupt me, and then make me do something about it. Like the old seaman said, "We have to go out, but we don't have to come back." We can put our lives and our reputations on the line. The surprising thing is that many unexpected people will get in line behind you when you show courage for Christ. The church and the world are waiting for someone to sound the alarm and shout, "forward, march."

We are in a battle for the souls of people. This is no game, no dress parade, no walk through the park, no casual encounter. It is a war against the powers of darkness and the forces of evil. The problems of our times have taken us beyond nice buildings, cheap grace, and mere ecclesiastical programming. It's time to strengthen resolve, firm up fortitude, and toughen tenacity. The world is going to hell at breakneck speed. God's judgment and the consequences of sin already have fallen on our culture in many places. But we are the agents God has raised up to change it for His glory and for the good of the souls around us.

These three short prayers will change your life forever. Here's what God thinks will help us win the war in which we find ourselves:

God is strong, and He wants you strong. So take everything the Master has set out for you, well-made weapons of the best materials. And put them to use so you will be able to stand up to everything the devil throws your way. This is no afternoon athletic contest that we'll walk away from and forget about in a couple of hours. This is for keeps, a life-or-death fight to the finish against the devil and all his angels. Be prepared. You're up against far more than you can handle on your own. Take all the help you can get, every weapon God has issued, so that when it's all over but the shouting, you'll still be on your feet. Truth, righteousness, peace, faith, and salvation are more than words. Learn how to apply them. You'll need them through your life.[2]

We already know God is going to win.

Service Must Be Seasoned with Love

Let me tell you what Pop London taught me (H.B.) about love. My grandfather, A.S. London, was a Sunday School evangelist who crisscrossed the American continent in the interest of Sunday School evangelism and church growth. He preached in hundreds of churches. His goal was always to have the largest Sunday School in the history of the local church on the last Sunday of his revival there. And he usually succeeded.

Early in my ministry, my grandfather lay dying in a Houston hospital. Diagnosed with leukemia, he did not have long to live. I was headed for the East Coast for a speaking assignment, so I took the red-eye to Houston to be able to spend a day with Pop London.

I arrived in Houston early in the morning and took a taxi to his hospital room. The halls were quiet, and my footsteps echoed as I walked down those corridors to find my grandfather's room.

As I looked into his eyes, we both realized this would probably be the last time we would ever be together on earth. That day was one of the most emotional days of my life. Pop was too weak to talk much, but we both enjoyed being together. I sat on the edge of the bed, held his hand, and told him how much his life had meant to me. I reminded him that he had always been there when I needed him.

Soon the day came to an end. I had to leave. I had been telling him all day how much I loved him and how much I would miss him. I remember saying to him before I had to leave, "Pop, you know that you and I will never see each other again this side of heaven. I just want to thank you for the great contribution you've made to my life. I want to thank you for the example you've been to me. I want to be just like you someday."

In the quiet of those last moments together, I said, "Pop, I'm just getting started in ministry. I've already made lots of mistakes, but as I've watched your life, I've seen how everybody seems to love you so much. You seem so confident, and you know how to make people feel important. Pop, what's your secret? What can I do to be like you?"

Even though he had been a great hulk of a man, Pop was now so weak he could hardly speak. He weighed less than a hundred pounds and his voice was very weak. I watched his eyes fill with tears. He took my hand and held it as tight as he could. Then he said softly, "Junior, remember, it is one thing for you as a minister to let people know how much God loves them. It is quite another thing for them to know how much you love them."

I will carry those words to my grave because they shaped my ideas about ministry. They represent the true meaning of servanthood: "It is quite another for them to know how much you love them."

We challenge you to be that kind of loving servant in your church. Love will win the war against all the principalities and powers. Your authentic servanthood will even attract those who do not seem interested. It will give you more satisfaction than you can possibly imagine or dream. And this is the only war in human history where its soldiers become better, sweeter, and holier.

Pop London was right. Loving service is a boomerang; the more you give it away, the richer you become.

RENEWAL STRATEGIES FOR CHURCH PILLARS
Finding Satisfaction in Service

1. View Christian service as a privilege and honor.

2. Fight your tendency toward apathy with vital faith.

3. Value service opportunities as more than holding an office.

4. Gain a sense of holy adventure from doing something that is too big to accomplish in your own strength.

5. Serving others impacts all relationships in the church.

6. Serving questions our notions about status.

7. Receiving benefits from service by others is sometimes difficult for those who lead.

8. Serving is usually unspectacular.

9. Serving really means love in action.

10. Serving provides spiritual growth opportunities for those who serve.

"*I see us going home to our churches and asking our pastors for permission, praying fervently for the favor of God, to stand before the congregation and say, 'Things are going to change around here. We're going to start to lift up our pastor. We're going to start to stand in the gap for our preacher. We're going to pray around the clock! We're going to build this pastor up. We're going to take him where he has never gone before.' I see us exploding in our churches.*"

*Bill McCartney,
founder of Promise Keepers*

6. 49 WAYS TO SHOW LOVE TO YOUR PASTOR
How to Use the Big A's

Lord of our church,
Thank You for the ministry family who serves our church.
We praise You for their insights,
> *their faith,*
> *their sacrifices,*
> *their training,*
> *their devotion,*
> *their faithfulness.*
Teach us a thousand new ways to show our love.
Help us to let them know how influential they are in our
spiritual development. We cherish them for their work's sake. Amen.

Businesses, large and small, are discovering how much CEOs, vice presidents, janitors, and all workers in between need the big A's— affirmation, appreciation, and admiration. Every human being needs a generous proportion of all three. And these expressions of affection are especially needed for and from persons with whom we work, live, and serve, especially pastors.

Interesting results take place when the three A's are sincerely expressed in business environments. More quality work gets done. Employees enjoy their jobs more, fewer mistakes are made, and workers move less often to other jobs. Personnel problems go down and absenteeism declines. In caring businesses, more customers trade with these firms and more products are sold. Maybe the business world has discovered something the church needs.

The big three A's—affirmation, appreciation, and admiration—also work wonderfully well in marriages and families. One blustery, take-charge-type father claimed he never needed admiration or thanks, but he melted when his three-year-old daughter said, "You are the best daddy in the whole world." That same tough guy feels so special when he affirms his wife as mother, wife, and best friend. And he goes off to his job in the morning singing when his wife says, "You are the best husband any woman could ever have."

Using the Three A's at Church

Affirmation, appreciation, and admiration all work well and are greatly needed in the church. In many congregational settings, insightful lay church leaders wish a "three A's" climate existed or could be cultivated, but they don't know how to start. Others don't miss it because they have never experienced it, but they will like it when they do. Though many people realize how important the three A's are, for some strange reason we find it hard to build strong acceptance and love into our church relationships, especially in communication to spiritual leaders from lay leaders.

Cherishing is in short supply in too many congregations. Without considering strengths, we tend to overemphasize shortcomings. We are often quick to judge and slow to praise. Too often the 1 percent rule controls. This rule focuses on 1 percent of what is wrong and misses the 99 percent of what is right. For example, perfect attendance for fifty Sundays is often overlooked when a person misses two services. One sentence in a sermon gets belittled without considering the good said before and after the troubling part. Having a bad teaching day, a Sunday School teacher may be criticized for a poorly presented lesson while many years of devoted, effective service is ignored.

All these situations can be bettered with the three A's. A grand place to begin this effort in your church would be to go out of your way to cherish your pastor. With imagination and effort, you can set in motion many ways to build a cherishing environment for your spiritual leader. Think of the agreeable results. Likely he will relish ministry more, will be more effective, and will stay longer in a pastoral assignment. In return, you and your church will enjoy working with a fulfilled servant of God. Then, your church atmosphere will radiate love and wholeness as suspicion, criticism, and adversarial relationships are minimized or forgotten.

Could it be that the Head of the church is promising lay leaders, "If you will befriend My servant and give special attention to his personal and family needs, I will bless your church in ways you never imagined, and you will enjoy your efforts in my church more"?

Before specific strategies for expressing appreciation, affirmation, and admiration are discussed, consider these principles:

• *Authentic.* Affirmation should be positive and true without a hint of what someone called "negative/positive." One lay leader who intended to honor his pastor said, "Even though some have had problems with our pastor, I love him dearly." That comment is veiled hostility, which does no good.

• *Unrehearsed.* Spontaneous affirmation carries more weight than planned speeches. Of course, both spontaneous and planned affirmations are needed. But this principle simply nudges every Christian leader to cultivate a spirit of gratitude and generosity so it becomes natural or even instinctive.

• *Genuine friendship.* Affirmation means more when it comes from a friend or from someone who wants to be our friend. The power of kindness is stronger when it comes from those with whom we have the closest relationships. Those who know the pastor best and work closest with her should express their appreciation and affirmation first and most frequently.

• *Do something.* An act of kindness carries more weight than a thousand words. Since it is our nature as Christians to want to serve, this principle should be easy for us to believe and achieve.

• *Move beyond the "1 percent" rule.* Affirmation, appreciation, and admiration are easier to express when we purposefully deny the 1 percent rule. There is much more in every person to affirm than there is to criticize. Let's face reality—no pastor or lay leader is right, courageous, or effective 100 percent of the time. If we focus on the 1 percent rule, we will never speak words of affirmation.

• *Everyone needs praise.* Even those who deny their need of affirmation need it. One old saint was praising her pastor for his faithfulness to the shut-ins. He embarrassedly replied, "I'm just doing what I want to do. Besides, it's my duty. Please don't praise me for doing my duty." After a few moments of thought, the old saint replied, "Pastor, if you don't need affirmation, why do you seem to enjoy it so much?" Even the most capable, apparently self-sufficient leader never outgrows a need for affirmation and appreciation.

• *A two-way street.* Affirmation, appreciation, and admiration are like a boomerang that helps the person who gives affirmation fully as much as it helps the one who receives it. In some strange way, giving affirmation makes one feel more fulfilled as a person. We are often too busy, too preoccupied, or too stressed out to realize that the recognition we give enriches our lives too.

• *Good gossip.* Positive secondhand affirmation will be reported on a church gossip line nearly as quickly as a negative report. It's fun to say something affirming about a pastor to a layperson and then wait to see how long it takes for him to tell the pastor. It usually happens pretty quickly. In the process, the initiator, the receiver, and the reporter are all encouraged. Management consultant Janis Allen says, "When someone says something good about another person and I tell that person about it, she seems to get more reinforcement value from it than if she had received the compliment firsthand."[1]

• *Attractive magnetism.* Appreciation for your pastor often attracts outside persons to church. They are more easily drawn to a congregation that speaks glowing, kind comments about their pastor. Outsiders who hear you speak affirmatively about your pastor become verbal though inexpensive advertisement for your local church and for the cause of Christ.

• *Love multiplies.* Many contemporary churches need a revival of love. They need to love Christ more, love each other more, love the world more, and be more loving to their leaders. A good place to start is to put new emphasis on loving your pastor as he serves Christ and you. Love is contagious and transmissible. Many congregations find they increase love by starting with their pastor and family. The pastor in turn starts loving the congregation more. Members of the congregation follow these leads, and before long the church becomes a fellowship of love and acceptance.

• *Match affirmation to the individual.* Give gifts of appreciation with the individual's preferences, values, and tastes in mind. A golf putter, even an expensive one, will not make much difference to one who does not play golf. And a new hunting rifle may not be much good to one who hates hunting for sport.

• *Make a memory.* The three A's work best when the recognition creates a story or memory the pastor can tell his family, fellow pastors, and young ministers for years to come. More creative readers of this chapter might ask their pastor to point out strategies in this chapter that would inspire him.

• *Match affirmations and achievements.* Ten years of pastoral service deserves different depths of affirmation than one year's service. Three years of heavy responsibility in developing a church plant or four years in a church building/relocation project are examples of activities that stand worthy of generous recognition of a pastor.

• *Err on the side of generosity or extravagance.* Too many people economize in their affirmations and gift giving. When giving a gift, go to the top or middle of the line rather than to the lowest possible price. A quality necktie might be more treasured than an inexpensive shirt.

• *Do it now.* Follow your heart and express it now. Do not allow good intentions to get away before turning them into deeds of love and kindness. Expressing the three A's is a good practice for the official group of your church, but it can also be done spontaneously and joyously by individuals.

The 49 Ways

No matter if you have been your pastor's thorn in the flesh for years, you can change. No matter if you have been one who draws stamina and strength from a pastor but never returns anything, you can start providing emotional and spiritual support for your pastor. No matter if you think of your pastor as being a rock of spiritual strength who needs nothing from anyone else, you can become an affirmer of your minister. No matter if you are a veteran grumbler about pastors whom you expect to be better, nobler, and more holy than you, you can change. Or if you have never thought to encourage your pastor, you can start now.

Anyone in any of these categories, or others we have not mentioned, can turn good intentions to loving deeds by using some of these 49 ways to express affirmation and appreciation to one of the most influential people in your life.

1. Speak up. Say something wonderful to affirm your pastor. You can do it following every expression of his competence and commitment to your church. Mention the sermon when you greet the minister at the door following a service and say, "Thank you for so many new thoughts and for the passion with which you preached them."

2. Write it down. A short, handwritten, first-class note that arrives on the pastor's desk by Tuesday or Wednesday is a thoughtful way to keep your pastor aware of what his Sunday ministry is doing for you. Or simply write a note following a demanding funeral, saying, "The Lord really helped you with a tough assignment. I'm glad you are such a sensitive pastor. I am proud of you." It always means more when people take time to write their affirmations, even those they have already given verbally.

A creative lay leader in a Southern California church writes a word of appreciation on a copy of Sunday's bulletin and pushes it under the door of the pastor's office. One teen in North Carolina does the same thing with Sunday's bulletin but puts the note under the windshield wiper of the pastor's car.

3. Appoint a spokesperson. Ask the pastor to allow a member of the congregation to make an announcement during a public meeting, and use that time to praise your minister. The spokesperson should be a respected leader of the congregation. A recent survey of American workers found that 63 percent of workers in the secular marketplace rate a pat on the back as an important incentive for future efforts; a public pat on the back will encourage your pastor as well.

4. Phone or fax the pastor. Call or fax your pastor with a word of thanks or affirmation. Fax machines and E-mail give parishioners new technology for expressing the three A's for their pastors.

Tell the minister, "Just wanted to tell you how much you are helping me grow spiritually." "I only called to say thanks and to let you know that you are helping me become more like Christ." If you get the answering machine, you do not have to ask for a return call; just leave a message telling your pastor you will be thinking about his positive impact on your life all week. Be as specific as possible with your words of praise. One woman prayed on the pastor's answering machine asking God to supply all her pastor's needs and some of his wants. Power in prayer is greatly multiplied when a person hears you pray for him by name—that doesn't happen to pastors often.

5. Give credit. When discussing an idea that originates with the pastor, be sure to give her credit. You can say, "I have been thinking a lot lately about an idea the pastor shared with us months ago. At that time, I was a little cold to the proposal, but I now see how important it is."

6. Name something after the pastor. One church named its new sanctuary after its pastor. Another congregation honored their pastor by naming the boardroom after him. A couple in Tennessee named their first child after their pastor—what pride she felt. A church in Maine gave a scholarship to a deserving student in the pastor's name; the idea was so well received, they established a permanent scholarship for future students from their church.

7. Improve the pastor's working environment. Nearly every pastor's office or study needs to be upgraded or expanded because of a lack of bookcases, insufficient filing cabinets, out-of-date office equipment, or old, battered furniture. Most ministers will do better if provided an inviting environment for doing good work.

If a faithful pastor spends the major part of his time in his study, is it too much to expect that it be comfortably furnished and cheerfully decorated? Furnish the study the way the pastor prefers rather than the way some committee decides. While many churches might not be able to afford to bring the office up to date in a week or a month, nearly every church could do significant upgrades over a year's time. An extra filing cabinet is a small price for making a pastor feel cherished. A new desk is a modest expenditure when it makes a pastor feel good about his work and his acceptance in the congregation. Why not make your pastor's work space the nicest office in the neighborhood and the most functional room in the church? Many people, if given the idea, would help raise money for this purpose outside the regular budget.

One church fussed and fumed about the pastor installing a phone in his car. The price was about $20 per month, but they lost hundreds of dollars of good will and wasted energy in the feeling of rejection the pastor experienced. Obviously, a church can't always provide everything a pastor would like, but on reasonable expenditures, it is advisable to provide them because of the good will and satisfaction that follow. Then everyone wins. Try thinking the way the minister thinks about his workplace and give him tools to do his work effectively.

8. Celebrate birthdays and wedding anniversaries. The spouses of employees are usually not a significant and visible part of the work climate in secular professions, businesses, and government jobs. The church is different. Feature and highlight your pastor's mate and family; love them into greatness.

Once a pastor asked a budding pianist, the son of an evangelist, to give a classical concert in his church. The program was a glowing success. In a few days, the evangelist faxed this note, "Anyone who loves and accepts my son is immediately loved, accepted, and appreciated by me." The lesson here is for a congregation to give extraordinary care and affection to the pastor's family on special days and to celebrate their important achievements.

9. Promote Pastor's Appreciation Day. Focus on the Family has led the way by issuing a national call for congregations to honor pastors each October. The reports from pastors about how they feel cherished and special are beautiful and inspiring.

Make this a new tradition in your church. When the idea is announced and promoted, many in your congregation will find some unique way to express affirmation for the pastor. As one teenage football player remarked, "Next to my family, Pastor Gregory is the most important person in my life. It's time we showed him how important he really is."

10. Send flowers, balloons, or plants. Even though most people think flowers are exclusively for women, try sending flowers to the pastor's home, especially on Christmas and Easter or "just for the love of it" day. A flowering plant delivered to the pastor's home in the dead of winter creates a never-to-be-forgotten memory. Remember, compensation is what your church pays your pastor for doing his job, but recognition is what you do to show affirmation, affection, and appreciation.

11. Plan Anniversary Sunday. Some churches have a tradition of celebrating the years of their pastor's service to their church on the anniversary of his first Sunday there. Many African-American churches do this especially well. Someone in the leadership group needs to be given responsibility for implementing this idea.

One Florida church buys its pastor a gift certificate to the best men's store in the area so he can purchase a new suit each year. Imagine how many times during the year someone comments on his suit and how he beams with pride when he says, "My wonderful congregation bought this suit for me."

12. Go overboard at Christmas. Often Christmas is a lonely time for a pastoral family, especially after all the activities of Christmas Sunday are over at the church. Pastors may feel loneliness at Christmas because they live too many miles from extended family to visit during the Christmas season; meanwhile, church families are busy with their own festivities.

A special way to honor your pastor at Christmas is to write a generous amount into the church budget and then supplement that amount by asking everyone in the congregation to give to a special Christmas offering. When those two income sources are combined, any church can give its pastoral family generous Christmas gifts. A Scrooge-type griper remarked, "We pay our pastor, so we don't need to do much at Christmas." To which a generous person replied, "Our gifts have nothing to do with pay and everything to do with love."

A Florida church Neil once pastored had a tradition of putting individual money gifts into Christmas cards for their pastors. One Christmas, the pastoral family received $750 in individual Christmas cards. Love makes us into givers and blesses the one who gives.

13. Honor achievements. One Colorado church had a celebration beyond all celebrations when their pastor was ordained. Many members drove a ways to attend the ceremony and then had an all-church celebration the next Sunday to honor their pastor's ordination. They took pictures of the ordination event, had the photos enlarged, and displayed them in the foyer.

Another church built a memory when they learned their pastor had completed thirty years in ministry. This congregation in the

South honored their pastor with a great banquet to which congregation and community people were invited. Videotapes were played and messages read from former parishioners. What an evening they enjoyed, celebrating the faithfulness of God as expressed through their minister's work and service.

A church being served by a wonderful student minister had a great celebration when she graduated from seminary; in fact, the celebration was so gratifying that the young pastor decided to accept the church's invitation to continue as their pastor after she graduated. That congregation believes their affirmation turned into an investment in the quality of pastoral leadership they enjoy as this young pastor develops into a mature minister. They discovered that affirmation often pays more than it costs.

14. Use creativity and imagination. One management specialist remarked about affirming business leaders, "The way we see it, spending one dollar on something unique and clever is better than spending fifty dollars on something ordinary and forgettable." Translated into the practices of a church, that means leaders should be creative and use imagination. Your originality might include the use of computer banners, spoof certificates, free lunches, coupons for baby-sitting or shoe shines, balloons, and coffee mugs with affirmative sayings on them.

15. Present plaques and certificates. Many pastors have a whole wall of certificates and plaques in their offices. You might think a pastor would not enjoy more plaques or certificates. Don't kid yourself—the more the better. Every plaque and certificate reminds a pastor of the love and affection of someone at a particular point in his pastoral pilgrimage. Make sure the plaque is well designed, appropriately framed, and worthy of being hung in a place of distinction for years to come.

16. Create a hall of fame. Create a photo hall of fame where pictures of the present and all previous pastors are displayed. It will take a little work to secure pictures of former pastors, but it is a worthy effort and helps your present pastor feel cherished. It is a church's way of assuring their present pastor that he is as important to them as anyone who has ever served here.

17. Surprise Post-it Notes. Write five or more Post-it Notes and leave them in conspicuous places on your pastor's desk, in his brief-case, in the front of his Bible, and in his car.

One thoughtful laywoman carries yellow notes in her purse and writes a note of thanks for Sunday and places it on the door of the pastor's study at church, or she sometimes places it on the pulpit just before the next service. Once she put a note in his pulpit Bible; she thought he preached even better that day, and he probably did.

18. Host appreciation dinners. Organize your lay leaders so one couple hosts the pastor and spouse for an appreciation dinner once each month. Set a regular monthly date so the pastor can schedule it several months in advance. Ask each host couple to cover the cost of the dinner, and provide a budget from the church so each host couple can purchase a small gift for the clergy couple, to be presented at the monthly dinner. These dinners might be done for only one year lest they lose their specialness.

19. "Did you know you are making a difference?" As a surprise to your pastor, ask each member of your decision group to come to your next meeting with a brief statement entitled, "How Our Pastor Is Making a Spiritual Difference in Our Lives." Ask those who write the statements to be as specific as possible. Because every pastor wants to make a difference, this exercise in affirmation will create a spiritual and emotional bond between your pastor and your decision group that you never knew could exist.

20. Flip chart thank-you. About twice a year, post a flip chart near the front entrance of your church where people can list thank-yous and appreciation for your pastor and his family. This is especially inspiring after some big achievement in the church or after some great loss has occurred, such as a number of people moving away, because an emotional letdown often follows. Those are good times to double or triple your affirmation and appreciation. The subliminal message is, "We are in this great work together, and you can count on us."

21. Provide magazine subscriptions. Magazine subscription prices have increased drastically in the last few years because of rising paper and postage costs. For this reason, most pastors cannot subscribe to as many magazines as they wish. Send your pastor a personal check for $25 to $50, suggesting the money be spent for new magazine subscriptions. Then every time the magazine comes during the year, she is prompted to feel cherished because of your thoughtfulness.

22. Surprise him with random acts of kindness. A few years ago, a lay leader from Nebraska was buying gas in a northeast Colorado convenience store along the interstate. He had just come from a great Promise Keepers rally in Boulder, Colorado led by Bill McCartney that honored pastors. At the gas pumps, the lay leader struck up a conversation with a stranger who turned out to be a pastor. The lay leader had never met the pastor before, but when he went into the station to pay for his own gas, in a moment of inspiration, he also paid for the pastor's gas. After the layman drove away and when the pastor started to pay, the station attendant told him his bill ($23.45) had been paid by the man who had just left. The pastor was so surprised that he wrote H.B. at Focus on the Family to say he had never felt so cherished in all the years of his ministry. What a grand return on $23.45. That pastor, for all the remaining years of his ministry, will tell that story over and over.

Think of a way to honor your pastor right now. What random act of kindness would he appreciate most?

23. Buy something for the pastor's hobby. One pastor has a model train collection, another has a stamp collection, another restores antique cars, another loves tennis, another works with wood, another loves golf, and another has a collection of preacher figurines. For each of those hobbies the pastor could use something he does not have. Listen carefully to what the minister says about his hobbies. Ask his spouse about what could be added. You can make a friend for life by simply buying a special tool or giving a needed accessory.

24. Secure tickets to special events. A pastor wants to take time off to attend the symphony. He never takes time to do so even though he could afford it and his wife wants to go. Why not buy them tickets for the best symphony concert of the season? Ask them to go with you. Make sure you arrange the time and date early enough so your pastor can plan the time in his schedule. His spouse will think you are the greatest for making this arrangement.

25. Provide a book budget. Most pastors have preferences concerning the books they would like to have to expand their library.

Many young pastors have a list of books they hope to buy in the future. If such a list exists, try to find out which one has top priority. If you can't get this information, purchase a gift certificate from his favorite bookstore. Every time your pastor uses that book for years to come, he will remember your kindness. Just today I used a commentary and a thesaurus given me by friends whom I remember with gratitude.

Since books are the tools of the pastor's profession—as needed as saws, hammers, and pliers for the carpenter—try to establish a book budget for your pastor. Even the more well-paid pastors are likely to need more books than they can afford. Though many churches will not be able to start with large amounts in this budget, start where you can and then increase the amount each year. Budgeting $75 to $100 per month is a good place to start.

26. Fund trips away. Though you may not be able to spend church funds for this purpose, why not ask three or four persons to help you fund two nights away at a place to be chosen by your pastoral couple? If they have young children or teenagers, arrange for the kids to stay with a church family who has children about the same ages as the pastor's children—a night out for the kids too. Be sure the couple has enough money to cover all expenses so the trip puts no strain on a limited budget. A pastoral couple will show their appreciation for months by doing better quality work, accomplished by two rested, cherished people.

27. Share a credit card. The pastoral family is about to take a vacation, and you know they are short of money. Why not give them the use of your credit card for five fill-ups? At $25 per fill-up, that amounts to $125. Most of us have spent that sum for something much less important in the past and will probably do so again. For churches who provide car allowances, they might wish to give the pastor full use of those credit cards when he is on vacation—an investment in a refreshed family to do even greater effective ministry during the next twelve months.

28. Push for self-care. Increasingly, our society is coming to understand that self-care of the human body and soul is one of the most important things a leader can do. Corporations sometimes buy "key executive" insurance that would pay large sums of money to the company if their key leader were to die. The insurance is a frank admission that the company depends greatly on certain leaders. Why not give attention to the health and spiritual well-being of your pastor by seeing to it that he takes care of himself? This means your pastor must take time away to recharge spiritual batteries, get needed exercise, and have regular medical care.

Spiritual self-care can be achieved by suggesting your pastor take one day per month away at a quiet place for reading, reflection, and renewal. The location could be someone's vacation home, a retreat center, or even a Catholic renewal center. Catholic renewal centers offer a quiet hotel-like room for prayer, reflection, and rest at a minimum cost; sometimes meals are even provided plus the use of a devotional library. Exercise renewal can be achieved by using a health club, playing sports, and taking advantage of a nearby church gym. Regular medical exams prevent larger health problems coming as a surprise.

29. Strategize early acceptance. When a new pastor comes to serve your church, see to it that strategies are in place so your pastor and his family feel instantly accepted. If the new minister is qualified to be chosen as your pastor, he is worthy of full acceptance without reservations. Of course, members of your congregation may be grieving for the pastor who moved away, and some may even feel abandoned. But the new pastor is not responsible for these feelings. He desperately needs immediate acceptance to get started with ministry. Take this new family into your heart and home as soon as possible.

In the official decision group, design and assign specific acceptance strategies during the start-up phase. If you brainstorm about this need in your decision group, you will be amazed at the many ways people are eager to help.

30. Suggest books from related fields. Many books in fields outside the pastor's regular reading requirements may be useful to her. Since it is difficult for a pastor to keep up-to-date in reading in her field of interest, she cannot be expected to know about books in other fields such as yours. Business, management, biographies, and social issue books will do much to enrich the pastor's thinking and preaching.

31. Make sure the housing arrangement is fair. If the church owns a parsonage, be sure regular attention is given to the upkeep of the property. If the parsonage is the worst-kept house on the block, it gives the wrong testimony for the church. Ask a new pastoral family what they would like to see changed in the parsonage. Replacing carpets, even before they are completely worn out, is a lot less expensive than moving bills for a new pastor. These questions usually should be directed to the pastor's spouse, especially if she is the family nest-keeper. Unworn orange shag carpet doesn't make for a happy living environment for the pastor's family. An outspoken church controller in a congregation in a nearby state who said, "We can't afford to replace the carpet in the parsonage" was met by a young professional woman in the decision group who said, "We can't afford not to!"

If the church provides a housing allowance, be sure the dollar amount is adequate. (If the church owned a parsonage, it would likely pay all the costs plus utilities.) Remember, when pastors are given the option to own their own homes, they usually stay longer.

Someone will raise the equity issue by asking, "If we give the pastor a housing allowance, the church will not gain the equity." Such a comment can be addressed with a counter–question, "Would you want the people you work for to own the equity in your home? If you worked for IBM, would you want the corporation to collect your equity so that when you retired, you had no funds for housing?" Fairness and generosity are the standards for deciding these issues.

32. Take a surprise gift to the pastor's home. Do a small act of kindness planned especially for the pastor or the family, like bringing a plate of freshly baked chocolate-chip cookies, a loaf of hot bread, a fruit basket you made up, fresh melons from the country fruit stand, a jar of jelly, or a fat pumpkin at Halloween season to their home. One lay person goes by the Christmas tree lot as soon as the trees arrive and pays in advance for the pastor's tree and then advises the minister and his family to go choose any tree they want.

33. Purchase car wash coupons. In many cities, coupons for car washes can be purchased in advance. Of course, prices will vary according to location, but with this gift, the pastor remembers the kindness of the giver every time the car is washed and much of the time in between.

34. Organize a LifeSaver award. One church honored its pastor by giving him two dozen packages of LifeSavers and called the presentation the LifeSaver Award because he had worked in a multiple-staff church for three months without a much-needed staff member. The executive committee of the decision group then took the pastor and the new staff member to a fine restaurant for lunch. The pastor kept the LifeSavers on his desk and offered them to people who came to see him. Of course, he commented on their significance to everyone to whom he offered a LifeSaver; that's a lot of positive feedback for a small expression of appreciation. The new staff member also felt cherished by this creative gesture.

35. Do something no one thought about before. Arrange a hot air balloon ride, provide a round of golf; rent a red sports car for the pastor to drive for a month; individualize a mug with the pastor's picture on it; print his picture on T-shirts for his family; arrange for a cruise; present a certificate for a family portrait for the minister's family; present a certificate for a night or two at a bed-and-breakfast; buy a newspaper ad or even a billboard ad with the pastor's picture on it that says, "Our pastor is loved."

36. Purchase a desk accessory. Get an accessory that the pastor enjoys using often. Here is how this idea affected pastors we know: A desk clock given by a church committee assures one pastor he is loved. An upscale letter opener and scissors, used several times every day, provide a happy remembrance of a Sunday School class who gave the gift. A picture frame given by church members reminds another pastor of the love of those friends and displays a picture of his family—two happy memories for the price of one. A leather desk mat reminds the pastor of a family he served during a loss of a loved one.

37. Organize a testimonial potluck. Too often testimonial dinners are left until retirement or times of resignations or leaving. Why not organize a testimonial dinner every year or two where persons are asked to give specific instances where the pastor served them? Someone from the decision group might express appreciation for an annual list of ideas, programs, and ministries the pastor made possible in your church. Because your pastor's impact on your church is so significant, it needs to be recognized in front of the entire congregation from time to time.

38. Make the pastor's family feel special. Think of creative ways you can affirm the pastor's spouse and children. List their accomplishments in the newsletter or post them on the church's bulletin board. Personally congratulate the child or spouse for their achievements. Let them know you love them and think they are special.

Sharing a pastoral parent with the church places unique demands on the children even as it provides them with unusual privileges. Many grown children of pastors give up on the church because of some unfortunate experience during childhood. All of this could be avoided or even forgotten had the congregation intentionally showered love on the children. Whatever the age of the children, make sure they know they are cherished.

Children at home can be affirmed every Sunday when you see them at church—"you look wonderful," "your family is a great example to our church," "everyone thinks you are special." One grandparent couple in a church we served gave our children a dollar bill nearly every time they met the children in church—two children multiplied by about fifty Sundays per year meant this couple gave our children about $100 a year. Our sons, now grown men, still have happy memories of that couple. Someone in the church once criticized this couple for giving children money: "You are buying their love," they complained. The generous couple responded, "We would rather buy their love than have them think we didn't love them."

Children in college can be remembered with letters, cards, care packages, and small gifts. Grown children can be invited back to the church for special events. Help the pastor's children know that you appreciate the fact that ministry is so often a family affair.

39. Brag on the pastor to his family. One innovative corporation sends a letter of praise to an employee's family at the end of a long or hard work project, thanking them for their support and acknowledging the important work their family did for the company. Why not send a similar letter once or twice a year to your pastor's family?

40. Institute the Golden Rule. See to it that your pastor is treated as well by the church as you would want to be treated by your employer. Too often in the church we think of pastoral leaders as doing their duty and as being expendable if we disagree with their decisions. Take care to see that your pastor is treated fairly in regard to time away, vacation time, working hours, compensation, and raises. In too many settings, the pastor is forced to carry the financial load when a church faces economic downturns that have nothing to do with him. Create a climate in your decision group and in the congregation in which your spiritual leader will always be treated with generosity and fairness.

41. Provide a personal computer and/or copy machine. Computers and copy machines are wonderful tools for sermon preparation. Even pastors who know little about office technology should be encouraged to see all the ways these two tools can assist them in their preparation and research. After a little investigation and training, most pastors will forever appreciate the day they were urged to step into the computer age.

42. Put a little money where your heart is. Put ten or twenty dollars in a birthday card addressed to your pastor.

One couple in a Florida church paid for six months of piano lessons for the pastor's children when they learned their church-planting pastor could not afford the lessons. A congregation whose church and parsonage were located in a radically deteriorating neighborhood with inferior schools paid the annual tuition for the pastor's children to attend a quality private school.

43. Give a food gift. One year, a pastor received three turkeys for Thanksgiving. Imagine his joy when he gave two of them away saying, "The generous people at our church gave us three turkeys and we wanted to share one with you." A nearly limitless variety of food gifts can be given to your pastor and family: out-of-season fruits like strawberries in winter, fruit-of-the-month clubs, seafood, jams and jellies, a variety of nuts, or candy. One farmer puts meat in the pastor's frozen food locker every fall. When someone takes you to a special place for dinner or bakes you some gourmet food, you remember it for years—so will your pastor.

44. Maintain a surprise gift box. Most of us frequently see small

130

items that remind us of our pastor. When you see those items, simply purchase them and place them in a box in your home for your pastor until you have accumulated six or seven of them. We have a friend who travels widely and shops valiantly; she keeps a box she calls her "Neil and Bonnie" box and fills it each year with things she knows we would love.

Examples you might consider are small books, Christmas tree ornaments, stationery, date books, calendars, pictures, key chains, note pads with appropriate sayings, candlesticks, bookends, mugs, picture frames, CDs, pocket flashlights, golf balls, tire gauges, small office supplies, or even a Swiss army knife.

45. Develop encouragement events. Statistics indicate that pastors most often decide to move or resign when they are discouraged about their ministry. This often happens when the church finances are tight, when attendance is low, when some crisis overtakes the church, or when a key person moves or dies. Then too there are many private issues that cause great concern that a pastor cannot discuss with a church member.

Since the effect of these events is usually obvious in a pastor's mood, this is an excellent time for lay leaders to plan an encouragement activity for the pastor. It can be a part of a regular monthly board meeting, a midweek service, or a planned bombardment of encouragement cards from people the pastor has helped in the last few months. One church leader in a Midwestern state arranged for five different persons to call the pastor with words of encouragement each day for a week; think how well that pastor must have preached the next Sunday. Later the minister joked that the program saved the church from having to locate a new pastor. Though he appeared to be joking, he was right on target. Pastors, like most other people, find it difficult to be effective, innovative, and spiritually alert when they feel discouraged, un-cherished, and unappreciated.

46. Offer to help. One youthful early retiree gives every Monday morning to performing any task at the church, run any errand, or visit anyone the pastor suggests. On Sunday afternoon or evening, he contacts the pastor to find out what his assignments are for the next day. He never resists what the pastor asks him to do—they both understand this is to help the pastor follow up on anything that is left over from Sunday. He even insists that he can save the minister time by doing personal things for the pastor, like making a trip to the post office, bank, hardware store, shoe repair shop, cleaners, or taking the car in for an oil change or wash.

47. Make dreams come true. Listen closely to the dream list of your pastor and his family. Some of their dreams can easily be accomplished with a small budget and a little imagination. One family dreams of two mountain bikes, or a trip to Disney World, or water skis, or two days at the beach. Appoint a scout to listen for clues, and then surprise your pastor by achieving his doable dreams.

48. Provide conference funding. Some of the most important new ideas for contemporary ministry are launched and explained at conferences. Ask your pastor which conferences he would like to attend. If she acts like attendance would be impossible, probe a little to find out the reason. The problem often relates to finances, so she is slow to tell anyone about the need. For example, a bi-vocational pastor may not be able to attend a conference because she cannot get the time off or she may not be able to miss the pay from the family budget for the time she is away.

49. Mission and/or Holy Land travel. Travel outside the United States is getting more and more common for ministers. Hundreds of pastors testify that their ministry was changed forever when they were able to give a week of service to a mission ministry outside the United States. Others will tell you that the Bible came alive in their preaching when they visited the Holy Land. Regrettably, these trips are usually thought to be impossible when a pastor has a young family or when he serves a smaller church. Instead of thinking it is financially out of the question, someone in your church should take the lead to see if it is possible. Often church members would be willing to give to finance such a trip if they knew of its significance and feasibility. Instead of talking about how impossible it sounds, check out the prices and ask about the programs. You may find it is less expensive than you first thought. Such a trip will create an enriching memory for your pastor that he will never forget.

49 Ways to Show Love to Your Pastor

It's Time to Begin

Lest we get mired in the details of how to show a pastor and family that they are loved, let's go back to the three A's—appreciation, affirmation, and admiration. For a pastor to stay the course, keep in the fight, and be spiritually strong, it is absolutely necessary that he know that the majority of the congregation is grateful for the impact of his ministry.

Several of these ideas for showing your love can be started immediately. Others can be initiated at the next meeting of the decision group. Though no church will do all of these things, every congregation can do something wonderful. Pastors who are loved work harder, stay longer, and feel more secure than those who are held at arm's length by lay leaders.

Show your pastor and his family that they are loved in tangible ways today. Besides being a wonderful thing to do, it will positively revolutionize the atmosphere of your church. It is a gift you give your pastor, but it is also a gift of new motivation you and your church will receive from your pastor.

Remember, a little praise goes a long way. Affirming, appreciating, and admiring your pastor is the best way to help him enjoy ministry for a lifetime even as it brings out the best initiative and loyal service from the man or woman of God.

Intangible Gifts Every Pastor Needs

Ministers cherish visible signs of love, and because of the message they communicate to pastors and their families, the giving of those gifts needs to increase. There is reason to rejoice because a fresh awareness of the need for clergy to be given affirmation and appreciation appears to be growing across the land. But an additional category of gifts is also needed. While these gifts cost no money, they represent high commitment levels by those who give them. These intangible gifts are highly significant because they create wholesome relationships and stimulate a Christlike spirit in the church.

To enrich yourself and your own service to Christ, try giving one gift from this list to your pastor each week. You probably will no longer need the list after a few weeks because giving these leadership

133

gifts has a way of becoming spontaneous and habitual. Check the list to determine what your gifts will be.

• *Purity.* Church pillars must live clean lives. Live by the biblical admonition, "Among you there must not be even a hint of sexual immorality, or of any kind of impurity, or of greed, because these are improper for God's holy people" (Eph. 5:3).

• *Trust.* Believe in your pastor with your whole heart. Overlook his faults. Build confidence for your pastor among your brothers and sisters in Christ. Refuse to listen to gossip or circulate suspicion.

• *Love.* Unlike the cheap love of the world, this gift is what one songwriter calls "the love of the Lord." It is an unconditional, volitional love that wants the highest and best for another. The pattern for this love can be found in the Apostle Paul's powerful charge, "Be imitators of God, therefore, as dearly loved children, and live a life of love, just as Christ loved us and gave Himself up for us as a fragrant offering and sacrifice to God" (Eph. 5:1-2). Esteem and affection between lay persons and their pastor are absolutely essential for doing ministry that pleases God.

• *Acceptance.* Being accepted by a congregation is a critical requirement for doing effective ministry. Sometimes a new minister is not accepted quickly enough because the congregation still grieves the loss of a former leader. But since everyone plans to accept the new pastor sooner or later, why not sooner?

• *Followership.* No one can effectively lead who does not follow. David McKenna's book title summarizes the issue, *Power to Follow and Grace to Lead.* Assure your pastor that you want to follow and that you are eager for her to authentically lead your church. Chaos and bedlam result without faithful followership.

• *Christ-centeredness.* From beginning to end, the church is about Jesus. He is the foundation and cornerstone. Without Christ at center, the church becomes a human institution that does good things, but it is not the church. To keep your minister encouraged, share your spiritual growth experiences with him. The spiritual development of persons like you is among a pastor's most significant sources of encouragement for effectiveness in the ministry.

• *Faithfulness.* Every pastor needs your faithful attendance, generous giving, and wholehearted loyalty. Such faithfulness is the foundation of all that is done in the local church. God's faithfulness is our model.

• *Fairness.* Integrity, kindness, fairness, and magnanimity all make the work of the church move ahead smoothly. When your sense of fair play is tested, ask yourself, "What would Jesus do?" Then do it.

• *Unity.* No one should expect 100 percent agreement in the church on every issue. But every church needs leaders who help create a bond of ministry that produces unity. Too much talk about differences always clouds the issues. Every church has persons who undermine unity. They should not allow themselves to be chosen as church leaders because the pressures are too great and their predictable responses are too destructive.

This list of intangible gifts could be expanded. You might add concepts like forgiveness, friendship, humanity, grace, humility, and benefit of the doubt. But an important point has been made—some of the most valuable gifts lay leaders can give their pastor or themselves is to be authentically Christian both inside and outside the church.

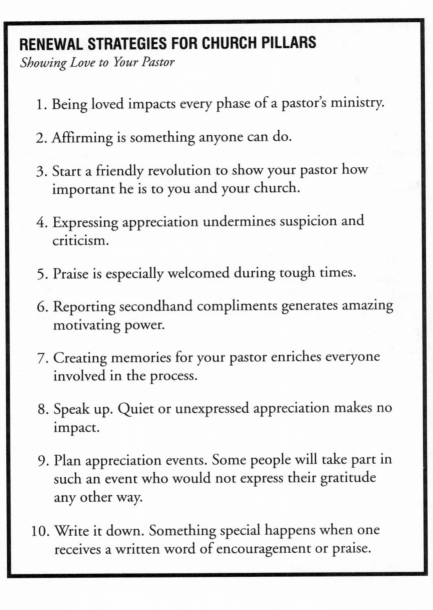

RENEWAL STRATEGIES FOR CHURCH PILLARS
Showing Love to Your Pastor

1. Being loved impacts every phase of a pastor's ministry.

2. Affirming is something anyone can do.

3. Start a friendly revolution to show your pastor how important he is to you and your church.

4. Expressing appreciation undermines suspicion and criticism.

5. Praise is especially welcomed during tough times.

6. Reporting secondhand compliments generates amazing motivating power.

7. Creating memories for your pastor enriches everyone involved in the process.

8. Speak up. Quiet or unexpressed appreciation makes no impact.

9. Plan appreciation events. Some people will take part in such an event who would not express their gratitude any other way.

10. Write it down. Something special happens when one receives a written word of encouragement or praise.

"Since Jesus Christ, the Son of God, took upon Himself the role of servant, so must we. The One who could have been or done anything, consciously and voluntarily, chose to be One who served, One who gave."

Charles R. Swindoll

7. SEVEN HABITS OF HIGHLY EFFECTIVE CHURCH PILLARS

Straight Talk to Lay Leaders

Look into the deep places of my soul, Lord Jesus.
Cleanse me from love of power and lust for status.
Make my service to Your church useful and blameless.
Shape my motives and actions into authentic Christlikeness.
Make me a lovable servant and a pleasing hired hand for You.
I want the love of Christ to radiate through my life. Amen.

The old "Pin the Tail on the Donkey" game is sweeping contemporary churches with a new spin. As if blindfolded, clergy and lay leaders alike pin criticism on the church without realizing the church is *us*—not them. As teenagers sometimes say, "Let's get real."

To increase the church's impact and multiply her effectiveness, renewal must start in congregations we serve and with individual believers like us.

There is a hopeful sign, however. Increasingly, pillars of congregations appear willing, even sometimes eager, to see the work of Christ reenergized. Such a trend must be fanned into a holy flame that moves from an abstract notion about revival to a concrete reality of renewal. Ecclesiastical governing bodies can't make it happen; too many people believe what these groups say makes no difference in individual congregations. A critical lay leader observed to a reporter in the hall outside a denominational legislative conference, "They don't do anything that makes any difference to the congregation I'm part of, so we don't care what they say.

And if we don't care, then certainly the world doesn't care." It's a lot like what a newspaper said recently: "The Pope is the darling of the masses, but few people pay much attention to what he says."

At the same time, it is obvious that secular culture cannot renew itself. If renewal comes, it must start with pillars in local congregations. To renew the church, lay leaders in the church must become more spiritually authentic, biblically faithful, and passionately aggressive for the kingdom. Renewal comes from Christlike behavior and determined resolve more than from lofty talk and endless good intentions.

As lay leaders fill this renewal gap in local congregations, a dynamic climate of flowering ministry will result. To make this a reality, individuals who influence and shape congregations must be absolutely honest in their assessment of their churches.

They must see what is broken and repair it or what is rusty and replace it. Since every congregation has its own attitudes, atmosphere, and priorities, it usually requires someone within the group to change a church. Thus, improvement or renewal most often comes from one individual's influence more than from any committee decisions.

Though conventional wisdom says one bad apple spoils a bushel, the church prospers more by living out the salty teaching of Jesus. A little salt preserves the whole. Though we may question whether a single individual can beneficially affect an entire congregation, the answer is yes.

Since a congregation is the sum total of her members' commitments and attitudes, it logically follows that each pillar has incredible influence to make a church better, nobler, and stronger. A healthy, nurturing environment can be started by one lay leader—try it.

A church near here has been battered for years by one aggressively controlling man. Almost singlehandedly, he caused three pastors to leave the ministry. Laypersons said their pastors should not pay so much attention to one person, but they did.

One key lay leader complained, "Pastors shouldn't let one negative, complaining person affect them." But ministers are always impacted by controllers and complainers. Ignoring the discouraging power of negativism is never easy.

Still another factor must be considered. In that church where one person caused so much grief, it's time for someone to intervene before another pastor checks out.

Why not become a Christ-motivated, revolutionary change agent who views your church in new ways? Consider how you can counteract and eliminate difficulties. What can you do to make your church more Christlike?

Remember as you form your strategy, a minister's greatest satisfaction is to build people up spiritually. Nothing brings a faithful pastor greater fulfillment than knowing lay leaders are growing in their relationship with Jesus Christ and together they are helping develop the congregation into a genuine New Testament church.

Just as marriage partners when they are the best mates possible give incredible gifts to themselves, the commitment to be an authentically Christian change agent becomes a magnificent gift you give yourself and your church. Everyone wins in the process. You delight your pastor's heart. You impact others with Christ's love. You undermine the influence of congregational wounders. And you enrich your walk with God. Your attitude, your commitment to Christ, and the joy of your faith help shape your church, edify it, and make your pastor enjoy the excitement of seeing people develop spiritually.

Every pastor dreams of leading a congregation like the church Luke described in Acts 2:44-47:

All the believers lived in wonderful harmony, holding everything in common. They sold whatever they owned and pooled their resources so that each person's need was met. They followed a daily discipline of worship in the Temple followed by meals at home, every meal a celebration, exuberant and joyful, as they praised God. People in general liked what they saw. Every day their number grew as God added those who were saved.[1]

Let's consider the seven habits that make lay leaders effective in the church while increasing their satisfaction with the journey.

Habit #1

Complete Devotion to Christ Start with the Basics

Luke describes the work of the early church as a congregation where members were devoted to Christ, to the apostles' teaching, to fellowship, and to the breaking of bread (Acts 2:42). Their devotion gave them a winsome attractiveness that drew outsiders and insiders to what they saw. It always works that way. Genuine commitment to Christ attracts people even when they do not understand the magnetism. The drawing power is wholehearted devotion to the Savior.

Such commitment to Christ charms and delights. Such devotion enriches your life even as it attracts others to the Lord and to the body of believers where you worship and serve. Veteran pastor and now U.S. Senate Chaplain Lloyd J. Ogilvie explains this attraction in a one-sentence description of the early church: "People wanted to be with those contagious, praising Christians and have what the Spirit had given them."[2]

All this leads to a sobering question every church pillar must ask at the quiet center of his or her personal faith: Does my walk with Christ make anyone want to know Him? Every congregation needs lay leaders who refuse to be distant, cold disciples of Jesus. That's an essential issue of lay leadership. Every clergy and lay leader must abandon unlovely harshness to become warm, compassionate imitators of Christ who love those He loves. Conversely, attempting Christian leadership without an authentic relationship to our Lord produces the worst kind of loneliness, creates inner emptiness, and repels people who haven't made up their minds about Christ.

Why not start inside your own spiritual depths by applying this poem by Dom Helder Camara to your own spiritual development:

The noise
  that prevents us hearing
  the voice of God
  is not,
  is truly not,
  the clamour of man,

the racket of cities,
still less
the stirring of the wind
or the whispering of water.

The noise
that completely smothers
the voice of God
is the inner uproar
of outrageous self-esteem,
of awakening suspicion,
of unsleeping ambition.[3]

Habit #2

Apply the Perspective of Jesus to Chuch Politics

As in other social organizations, politics is real in the church, in
denominations, and in parachurch organizations. A veteran minister
correctly observed, "Wherever two or more people live or work
together, you have politics, even in marriages." Deals are struck,
advantages are traded, control is grasped, and posturing is common
wherever people meet. We get caught in spiritual dead-end streets,
however, when we think church politics is God's will, especially when
it works for us. Politics cripples and incapacitates the church when
accommodations become more important than accomplishing the
mission of Christ. And that happens much too often in the contemporary church scene.

It is frightening how political power moves across aging generations so the idealism of youth drastically changes as they gain power.
Then, membership in the "in-group" seems more important than
accomplishing Christ's mission in the world. That's a destructive trap
for the church. This reality easily grinds church organizations to a
snail's pace or outright standstill because increasing energies and funds
are required to take care of "important" people.

Correctives are difficult, but they must be initiated. We can do a
lot to start church renewal by confronting corrupt systems with a call

to mission. Meanwhile, we must apply Jesus' principles to judge our own political attitudes and actions to be sure we are not part of the problem.

The holy work of your church will improve measurably if you admit church politics exists but refuse to manipulate it or be manipulated by it. Beware of church politics—they can become a fatal, faith-destroying disease that often starts with a tiny infection or a minor accommodation. This means every leader must examine his or her conduct against Jesus' teachings concerning genuine greatness. Our Lord taught and demonstrated by His life that servanthood was the path to effective service. His servanthood symbols were a basin, a towel, and dirty feet.

The spirit of Jesus can revolutionize church politics if the following correctives are applied.

• *Evaluate personal motives.* Thoroughly examine your motives when you think you would like to win an election or be given a high-profile assignment in the church. Is your purpose to accomplish Christ's mission or gratify your ego? You know, so does God.

• *Trust God.* Believe God to work through or around political structures. He can be expected to overrule even the most blatant, manipulative orchestrations of self-centered, crafty church politicians.

• *Be Christian.* Cultivate personal piety so your character is attractive, sought, and needed by the congregation. Refuse to play the political game, but be willing to serve when opportunities are presented.

• *Reform the system.* Intentionally gain status by serving with distinction so you can reform the church from within. Some of the saddest people are those who preside over corrupt structures they once scorned. Try to be like Abraham Lincoln, who vowed, if given an opportunity, he would stop slavery; he couldn't forget that vow when he became President. Ask yourself if you handle authority in a way that displeases God.

• *Promote compassion.* Take up the cause of downtrodden persons whom the church political system wounds. Every political system has casualities, lots of them. The more corrupt the system, the greater the number of good people it wounds.

• *Focus on the mission.* Speak up for the real mission of Christ's church at every opportunity. Self-interests and political efforts begin to fade when congregations focus on the mission.

• *Remember who you were.* If you are given or grab political power, remember how misused authority frustrated you when you were one of the "little people." Resist calling political manipulations the "will of God." Refuse to fool yourself into believing political half-truths about yourself and others. Stop making those speeches that others interpret, "It's God's will since it seems so good to me."

• *Check your competence.* If you are offered an assignment or asked to serve in a position where you have no skills or competency, decline. Suspect your motives or the processes of a system that give you an opportunity for which you have no gifts or skills. If you find you have a task for which you do not have skills or cannot acquire them, resign. God will likely be pleased with your action even if those in power don't understand. In any organization, especially the church, persons placed in assignments beyond their competency destroy morale and retard achievement. It's the secular Peter Principle of being promoted beyond competence, dressed in Sunday duds.

Habit #3

Talk Healthy Talk—Make Good Use of the Grapevine

Every church has a grapevine. You are part of it whether you know it or not. Church people love to talk. They often ask probing questions of those who know information so they can pass on what they gather. Then, a kernel of truth gets exaggerated. Church rumors usually focus on the pastor and those close to him. Often the informers use loose talk to put them in the spotlight. In grapevine discussions, accuracy is usually compromised simply because the talker seldom knows the facts.

Inaccurate information repeated over and over causes lots of mischief for innocent people. Deception and false conclusions plant seeds of confusion, distrust, and doubt—all destructive to any church.

Gossip can easily destroy a church's mission, and it often does. It encourages insensitivity to others, prejudges situations, persons, and causes, and encourages everyone to express radical or even unchristian opinions. Scripture explains the problems corrupt communication creates:

A word out of your mouth may seem of no account, but it can accomplish nearly anything—or destroy it. It only takes a spark, remember, to set off a forest fire. A careless or wrongly placed word out of your mouth can do that. By our speech we can ruin the world, turn harmony to chaos, throw mud on a reputation, send the whole world up in smoke and go up in smoke with it, smoke right from the pit of hell. . . . With our tongues we bless God our Father; with the same tongues we curse the very men and women he made in his image. Curses and blessings come out of the same mouth! (James 3:6-10)[4]

On the other hand, positive use of the grapevine can bless a church, fire its motivation, and encourage an atmosphere of accepting love. Regrettably, constructive informal communication is in short supply in churches. Perhaps this is because church members feel forced to spend so much energy putting out fires caused by misguided rumors. You can change that.

Begin by asking why church people talk so much. They may be intensely interested but lack information, so they talk to find out if others know more than they do. If this idea has validity, why not provide talkers with more information as a starting point for using the grapevine positively? For example, one recreational talker questions leaders in different settings and at different times; then like a private investigator, he adds up the details and becomes the resident informant who spreads the story. When you see this pattern, give the self-appointed investigator the information you want people to know. Then, let him talk.

Why not think of ways to make your church's grapevine useful? Why not put significant facts on the grapevine? It is wonderful fun to tell a positive story to a talker and then wait to see how long it takes the information to get back to you and with what embellishments. Sometimes the resident talker forgets who told him the story and repeats it to the originator. Sometimes the tale comes back in hours, but almost always within a few days.

Since people are bound to talk, why not give them something positive to discuss? Putting accurate messages on the grapevine is easier than duplicating them on a copy machine, recording them on someone's answering machine, or using E-mail.

Habit #4

Discover Guidance—Seek God's Direction

Guidance for life and service are promised in Scripture. Yet few decision groups diligently seek God's direction in the details of their work. When a crunch comes in congregational decisions, we tend to lean on our experience, logic, understanding, or opinion. How soon we forget how much anguish comes from doing what we want and calling it God's will.

In contemporary congregational life, an attitude prevails that everyone can express his opinion freely about anything, no matter how outrageous his position. Since democracy is so treasured in our civic life, we assume everyone has a right according to the First Amendment to speak his mind in church. The last word for the work of God, however, is not the prevailing group opinion or one's personal view, but God's will. Human opinion and wisdom must be subservient to God's will.

Thus, every decision group must seek to understand what God thinks about an issue. Scripture helps us find the divine will on questions of abiding principle. Divine guidance and the combined judgment of seriously committed Christian people help us find our way on other issues. The divine perspective can be made known to us through prayer, dialogue, or even checking church history on issues where the Bible seems silent. Admittedly, finding the will of God is sometimes difficult, but seeking such direction always reminds a decision group of its partnership with God.

A far greater difficulty, however, occurs when church decision groups do not even try to find the will of God. It can happen so quickly. Group members express their opinion or prejudices, a vote is taken, the majority rules, and the group moves on to the next item on the agenda. In this way of doing things, we may falsely assume the Lord's purpose for His church is the prevailing opinion of those present and voting. But God sometimes surprises us by siding with the thoughtful minority.

Every clergy and lay church leader remembers politically charged occasions when decisions were made in haste. God was not consulted with even one short prayer; no search of Scripture took place; and no attempt was made to quiet noisy personal opinions so God's directive could be heard. Often those events are later justified by calling them the will of God. Shamefully, some of these outcomes are so disastrous that it is laughable to blame God. One writer suggests calling our judgments "God's will" is like taking His name in vain.

On a purely rational basis, can anyone seriously believe God is pleased with congregational and denominational decision groups who operate His church according to their designs?

Perhaps a procedure should be instituted so decisions will only be considered when they are rooted in an honest effort to find the mind of God. A Scripture passage cast in contemporary language speaks soberly and thoughtfully about this issue:

> Real wisdom, God's wisdom, begins with a holy life and is char-
> acterized by getting along with others. It is gentle and reason-
> able, overflowing with mercy and blessing, not hot one day and
> cold the next, not two-faced. You can develop a healthy, robust
> community that lives right with God and enjoy its results only if
> you do the hard work of getting along with each other, treating
> each other with dignity and honor (James 3:17-18).[5]

Decision groups must commit to a simple reality that the church is local before it can ever be national, international, or parachurch. Ultimately, anything that needs fixing must be lived out locally before it is imposed or corrected on other levels of the church. God trusts us with leadership responsibility to see that this happens. James Sparks in his *Pot-shots at the Preacher* reminds us of the strange doings of God when He trusts His church to the likes of us:

> The care and feeding of congregations is truly a testimony to the
> mystery of God's ways as well as His sense of humor. Throughout

the ages, He has gathered His people into communities of faith and given them full responsibility for the treasures of faith. That God should choose to do this through congregations, so diverse and sometimes capricious, is a witness to His patience, love, and utter trust in humankind in spite of our inherent foibles.[6]

One truth is self-evident. The church's potential for renewal is usually found within the walls of the church and within the hearts of its members—seldom outside. When we listen to ourselves, our criticisms concerning the church sometimes sound like condemnation of government in Washington or the United Nations. In this confusion, we perpetuate the myth that our church will be more effective when somebody outside the fellowship does something. In reality, however, local church leaders have little influence to correct anything on national or international levels. But we can do everything in our power to see that our local congregation is pleasing to Christ, that it is guided by biblical priorities, that it is warm and accepting, that its will is set on fulfilling God's mission for His church in the world, and that it makes the main thing the main thing, with the assurance that doing the main thing for the main reason keeps a church spiritually fit and optimizes its influence.

Habit #5

Keep Yourself Growing Spiritually—Reap the Personal Harvest

Authentic congregational leadership starts and continues with an individual who cultivates a growing, personal relationship with Christ. In business and government, leaders are appointed or elected on the basis of training, experience, prestige, financial accumulations, or connections. But leadership in the work of God, from biblical times until now, requires stalwart Christian character as a bedrock foundation. Acts 6 records how the early church organized itself for greater efficiency by choosing leaders who demonstrated their faith and their wisdom and were full of the Holy Spirit. No mention was made of experience, brilliance, prestige, or standing in the community. And following their election to that group, Stephen and Philip found themselves in a frighteningly short time at the front lines of the spiritual battles of their time. Stephen was even stoned to death.

To keep yourself growing spiritually is to acknowledge that the foundation for all service in the kingdom is a vital relationship with Christ. That means you have met Him in a life-transforming encounter and continue to live in a vital relationship with Him and His people. You keep your soul robust through worship, prayer, and application of Scripture to your life. You purposely choose to embody the example of Christ in all you do and say. And you seek the mind of Christ in everything, especially in decisions you help make for the church.

While all this makes you qualified for leadership, it also provides you with a satisfying quality life. A wholehearted relationship with Christ, so much more than a mere cloak to make a leader appear pious, is the most essential ingredient for living a fulfilling life. Thus, you do not become a victorious Christian so you can be a leader, but you are a leader because you are an authentic Christian. Many people can lead secular organizations, but no one can effectively lead in a local congregation who does not have a personal relationship with Christ and continues to develop a Christlike character.

While on the surface this concept may sound like restating the obvious, in practice it shifts the focus of our leadership from doing to being, moves priority from the how of decision-making to the why, and transforms planning from the limitation of existing resources to finding miraculous ways of accomplishing a holy mission for God. Personal piety helps open a leader's vision to the holy work of the church.

History tells us that the church has had its most significant impact on the world when it was led by persons who were wholeheartedly devoted to Christ. That starts and continues through a leader's relationship to Christ. Thus, the first query to a potential leader must be, "Tell me how you met the Savior." And the second question is closely related, "How have you grown in your relationship to Christ since you started with Him?" A congregation cannot be an authentic Christ-centered church when led by persons who have only seniority, talent, money, and social standing. Above all else, the congregational pillar must know Christ.

Habit #6

Grow Past the Past—Dealing with Toxic Knowledge

Recently I renewed friendship with a wonderful lay couple who have served Christ for nearly a half century at the forefront of three or four congregations—always faithful, loyal, and generous. They announced they changed denominations because they were tired of years of disputes and conflicts. They are neither kooks nor off-center church consumers; those who know them confirm that they have always been peacemakers. With a calm, steady influence, they have quieted murmurings and grievances in the churches where they served. But the accumulation of toxic relationships has taken its toll and they feel the need for relief. Sadly, though they are not fully aware of it, they likely will find similar situations in their new congregation and new denomination because it is pervasive in the contemporary church.

Anyone who has been around for a while can identify with the seminary professor's description of the contemporary church. He observed, "The church is a lot like Noah's ark. You couldn't stand the stench inside if you weren't afraid of the storms on the outside." We nod in sad agreement, because the church where we serve needs to become something more than it has been. Let's admit that many people have given up on the church because it so often promises more than it delivers. It talks a holy game while being ruled by self-serving priorities. The church of the future must become much more than the church now is in so many places.

Every clergy and lay leader must do what they can to make the church nobler and more influential in our time. Meanwhile, as we work to make the church better, we must find ways to rid ourselves of toxic thoughts and do away with past hurts in our hearts. One preacher calls it "surrendering toxic memories". One old saint calls it "relinquishment." We dare not allow past poisons to undermine the church's present or abort her future. The way to free ourselves from these toxins is to apply Paul's advice to the Philippians to our own attitudes about the church:
- Rejoice in the Lord always.
- Be gentle to all.

• Give up your fretful anxiety about everything, including the church.

• Allow God's peace to guard your hearts and minds.

• Dwell on the true, noble, right, pure, lovely, and admirable.

• Reproduce in yourself what you have seen in spiritual giants. (Phil. 4:4-8, paraphrased)

An even stronger remedy for our poisonous toxins from the past shows up in the apostle's testimony:

I consider everything a loss compared to the surpassing greatness of knowing Christ Jesus my Lord, for whose sake I have lost all things. I consider them rubbish, that I may gain Christ and be found in him, not having a righteousness of my own that comes from the law, but that which is through faith in Christ—the righteousness that comes from God and is by faith (Phil. 3:3-9).

Habit #7

Try Seeing Your Church as God Does—Be Realistic

Ask yourself, "What do I pretend not to see?" It is easy, while trying to be a positive thinker, to refuse to see ourselves, families, or church as they really are. On the contrary, some people seem to have a need to see life, family, and church in the worst possible light. Both harmful extremes must be avoided. Let's admit no human relationship is ideal nor totally flawed. Let's understand it is human to try to ignore what is painful. At the same time, let's also remember that fooling ourselves about the church keeps us from initiating improvement. How, then, should we realistically view the church?

• *Cherish strengths.* How is your church uniquely strong? Is it the people, the history, the building, the location, or the spiritually mature people who make up the congregation? How can these unique strengths be used to make the church even stronger? What does your church do better than most other churches? What does your community think about your church's credibility?

• *Determine what improvements are possible.* Often lay leaders put off implementing an obvious improvement because every needed

152

improvement cannot be made. Prioritize what needs to be done. Consider what can be done with little effort and cost. For example, one church that meets in a multipurpose room at a school dramatically improved its worship space by turning the movable seats in the opposite direction. It took fifteen minutes to make a change that positively affected every worshiper. It would have been foolish to put off such an uncomplicated change just because funding prevented them from building their own facilities. Often doing some simple change helps a congregation see how they can consider making more major changes. Don't refuse to do what can be done immediately because you can't do everything.

• *Test your reactions.* When he was eight, one of my sons told me, "Whenever I ask you for something, you always answer no." As I thought about his reaction, I saw my son was right. Though my responses seemed grossly unfair to him, they were rooted in my Depression-era childhood. When I understood what made me respond the way I did, I worked at improvement so I could deal with issues more realistically. A similar improvement is needed in many churches. Ask yourself how you habitually respond to issues and if those responses need to change.

• *Question your denials.* Look for such phrases in your conversations as, "I always say" or, "I don't do that" or, "I can't believe you said that" or "If I were in their situation, I would never do that" or, "I didn't say that or, even think that." All these and similar phrases may be symptoms that you are not realistic about what is really important to you. Any phrase that turns responsibility to someone else and is slow to admit "it is me standing in the need of prayer" may be a denial of the truth.

There is a way of fooling ourselves so thoroughly and so frequently that we start believing falsehoods about ourselves and others. It shows when we take credit for what others do. It happens when we are more interested in establishing blame than correcting difficulties. It may allow resentment from the past to poison our present.

• *Forgive others as a gift to yourself.* Forgiveness, as it should be, is usually taught and preached as a Christian duty. But forgiveness is a wonderfully freeing gift you give yourself so you can move on with your spiritual development without being locked into a hurtful experience from your past.

Cherishing a past offense is an extravagance no one can afford. To do so may plateau your spiritual development and corrode your ability to live joyously. The Bible charges us to forgive in the same measure that we have been forgiven. That's a lot. We forgive because the Bible says so, but also because it makes us more whole human beings and conserves our spiritual energy for what really matters.

Other Habits God Can Use

In listing seven habits, a danger of leaving out significant characteristics is always present. The habit that is overlooked may be the exact characteristic you need to succeed as a Christian leader in your congregation. Thus, it is important to go beyond a list of characteristics and get to the essential Christ-shaped personhood of an effective church pillar.

Why not take up the challenge to be the best leader you can be by being the best Christian you can be? This challenge is to be more like Christ before you try to do more for Him. Your congregation needs all the skills, strategies, and solutions you can provide, but it needs your spirit, your commitments, and your spiritual growth even more.

A Christ-saturated life, at the most fundamental level, is the most important component of authentic kingdom leadership. Well beyond elections, budgets, and committee meetings is the impact your life makes. You can make a revolutionary, spiritual difference in congregational life by living according to the mandates of Jesus and by counting service as the highest privilege of your life.

Be the leader God can use. Be the leader people gladly follow. Take your share of responsibility for the spiritual well-being of your church by allowing God to shape and stretch you more and more into the image of Christ. Christlikeness draws others to Christ and produce incredible joy in you.

The power of God is promised to work through us: "Now to Him who is able to do immeasurably more than all we ask or imagine, according to His power *that is at work within us*" (Eph. 3:20, italics mine).

RENEWAL STRATEGIES FOR CHURCH PILLARS
Effective Church Pillars Must Be Growing Christians

1. Draw close to Christ to reenergize your leadership skills.

2. Renewal is often rooted in the Christlike actions of those who lead.

3. Revival often starts in the heart of a church insider.

4. Refuse to allow negativism to strangle your church.

5. Apply the perspective of Jesus to church politics.

6. Refuse to glorify political manipulations by calling them the "will of God."

7. Make positive use of the church grapevine.

8. Seek God's guidance in all church decisions.

9. Grow past the past.

10. Try to see your church as God does.

"We take our lead from Christ, who is the source of everything we do. He keeps us in step with each other. His very breath and blood flow through us, nourishing us so that we will grow up healthy in God, robust in love."

Ephesians 4:15-16
The Message

8. CREATING A HEALTHY CONGREGATIONAL SELF-IMAGE
Jesus Wants Every Church Healthy and Well

Lord of the church,

> *Make our congregation holy, healthy, whole.*
> *Saturate our labors with the image of Christ.*
> *Help us discern Your plan for the church*
> > *in this setting and time. Amen.*

Pastors almost always start serving a congregation with high hopes. They assume their church is actually a living cell of the everlasting Church of Jesus Christ. They believe their church is more than a regional franchise of a certain brand of Christianity, where customers must be pleased and the local outlet must show a profitable bottom line. They assume pastoral leadership of a congregation with enthusiasm and promise, expecting the church to be the people of God and the body of Christ. Many even believe their new assignment has potential for becoming their "dream church," where they will stay for the rest of their life.

All too often, however, those dreams soon turn into nightmares. Then like the pastors before them, they wait it out awhile. Soon they pack up their hopes and take their dreams to another place.

The situation is sad. There is no one to blame. Apparently, the status quo just happens even when no one wants it. But do we have to live with it year after year?

Like those who first settled America, many contemporary church pillars would rather be settlers than pioneers. Sadly, in settling down into no progress, avoiding controversy, and maintaining traditions, a local congregation begins to acquire a spiritual inferiority complex.

They ask, "What's wrong with us?" They wonder if the church will ever fulfill its mission. Low congregational self-esteem results. They think, *We are nobody. Nobody wants to be our minister. Nobody wants to attend this church.* Then as morale skids and inferiority increases, a congregation can easily forget who it belongs to and what God has raised it up to do.

For years, we have been intrigued by churches that are vital and vibrant, busy fulfilling their mission, and how different they are from those that stagger to maintain their existence. In the first group, we noticed one characteristic is evident in nearly every church: a "positive self-image," or a "healthy congregational self-concept," or a "wholesome self-esteem." Those congregations feel good about themselves, their work, and their future. A church with a strong self-image holds its head high. It has a lofty vision. It values its importance in the community. And such a church knows it is a vital part of the kingdom of God.

The Anatomy of a Low Self-Image Church

For illustrative purposes, let's go back a few years in H.B.'s ministry history to take an inside look at a tiny church whose congregational self-concept was significantly less than positive. In fact, he sometimes felt like the pastor who said about his church, "I would not consider attending this church if I were not the pastor."

H.B.'s first church had problems of location, appearance, and reputation. Nestled behind a service station on a side street in a second-rate section of the city, the church could not expect people to attend without some pretty good reason. And no one did.

Of course, everyone thinks a church's location has nothing to do with self-image, but it does. A poor location and a poor appearance send a negative message to all who pass the church, and that hurts.

But it also communicates a "we don't matter much" spirit to the faithful members who use the facilities week in and week out.

Every church location should send out signals of welcome, communicate Christlike love, and show signs of vibrant life. When real estate agents talk about desirable properties, the number-one thing they look for is "location, location, location." H.B.'s church was in an undesirable location and had languished in its setting for years.

Though the church's location could not be changed, the opinion of the location changed. It became a happening place. All of a sudden, the church site looked different to those who passed by. They saw people. They saw caring. They saw happy faces. The lights were on. Something important was taking place. When that happens a church can develop a healthy self-image even in a bad location. And a church, even with a good location, can have a bad self-image if nothing is happening that matters.

That little church had another problem—poor reputation. Even the denomination and neighboring churches looked down on that humble band in their less-than-ideal location.

Why? No one had gone to jail or stolen money. The problem was the people looked down on themselves. They had pretty well decided that they were a congregation of nobodies and that was the way it would always be. They asked themselves, "Who would want to come and join our group?" Their answer was, "Nobody." They thought, *We are just forced by our circumstances to stay here in our negative little world until we all die out.*

What a dreadful way to live, and what a horrible testimony for the cause of Christ.

A few weeks ago I (H.B.) was in Florida. There was a great contingent of Amish people on the beach. They were dressed in plain, dark clothing. The men were dressed in casual clothes, the women in long skirts, dark stockings, and head coverings. At first I felt sorry for them. *Why would they dress like that?* I thought. *Don't they know they are the laughingstock of the whole beach?* But then I noticed something very interesting. These folks were not the least bit intimidated by the surroundings or by the fact they were different. They were not ashamed. They were laughing and energetic. They didn't look to see what others were thinking. They were satisfied with their self-image and convinced of their lifestyle. It was a meaningful moment for me. In fact, I found myself saying under my breath, "Good for you! Nice going! I'm proud of you!"

You see, there are significant differences between the church I served and the group at the beach. It all has to do with how people felt about themselves. In a church, it has to do with how secure and comfortable we are with being what we are called to be and do.

The absence of purpose was the third problem area in H.B.'s first ministry assignment. That church had forgotten why they were there. So many years had come and gone without measurable results. They had grown content with merely existing. They reminded me of the man who got up early one morning before daybreak. He took his fishing gear and headed for a mountain stream. He walked out into the cold water with all the equipment like he was a seasoned fisherman. He had a hat filled with nicely tied flies. He had his waders on. He had a net. He had a basket around his waist to hold the fish. He had it all. Then after a few casts, his line was struck by a beautiful rainbow trout. He fought the fish awhile, and then reeled it in where he could use his net to capture his prize. As he stood looking at the fish, he was heard to murmur, "Can you beat that? I caught a fish!"

What did he expect? Didn't he go fishing? Didn't he prepare to catch a fish? Why would he be so surprised? Too many churches are like that. They never really expect to attract anyone, and if they do, they don't know what to do with them.

It does not matter what size your church is or how many pastors you have had. It's "fishing time." That's the purpose of the church—to fish for lost people. To cast out your net. To reach the lost. That is what Christ expects of you, and that is what He promised to empower you to accomplish.

Leadership was the fourth problem in that first church. There was no one to follow. The church had gone through so many pastors and had run off so many potential leaders that they moved around and around in circles, going nowhere. They were bogged down in their past. They had no one to help them get on course again. It was pitiful. No one wanted to make a decision. They were afraid someone would decide something that might create a long-term problem, so they did nothing.

I love watching TV nature programs. The migration of animals on the African plains always intrigues me. The wildebeest is at the top of my curiosity list. It's an ugly beast that is constantly on the move. It seems to never stop. To fight for survival, it travels hundreds of miles to find food and water.

Some churches are like that. We weep over congregations that are like wildebeest. No leadership. They exist from one Sunday to another. When the new year comes, they start over again—doing the same thing the same way because no one says, STOP! No one says, "Let's evaluate the way we do things." No one thinks to ask, "Could we do it better? Since nothing is happening, should we do it differently?" Some of those churches don't even know why they resist change, but they do. With no improvement or progress, their constant wanderings continue. The mission program is like it always has been. The order of the worship remains the same. The decision group does things the way they always have—and the list goes on.

As I watched the huge herds of wildebeests in Africa on their migration route, I wondered if it could have been any different for them. For hundreds of years, new generations have done it the same way. They probably could not change if they were forced to. But in thinking about the church, if it does not change its habitual wanderings, in time, like the wildebeest, it may simply die out, wear itself out in its wanderings, or be destroyed by predators.

The solution: find a leader or be a leader. Then lead, follow, or get out of the way so God can help somebody do something in your church.

There you have four problems that create a crippling congregational self-image, which is so frequently present in contemporary churches. But when those factors are identified and understood, they can be changed. Check the list again and immediately change what you can in your church.

• *Location.* It is not so much where a church is, but what happens there, how the facilities look, and how the congregation uses them.

• *Reputation.* Though reputation has to do with what others think of you, it is mostly how your congregation feels about itself.

• *Purpose.* It is not so much that you exist, but why you exist. Why has God providentially established your church?

• *Leadership.* It is not so much who is the leader, but if you are following the leader to a desired goal. Are designated leaders leading? And are leaders being developed to take the church to the next plateau?

Birthmarks of a Healthy Self-Image

I (H.B.) remember when my grandson, Taylor, was born. We were all standing around him, making sure he had all his toes and fingers. I noticed a very small birthmark on the inside of his left calf. I don't think anyone else noticed it but me. But I thought then, *Taylor will carry that little signature from God all the rest of his life.* He is six now, and at Thanksgiving when we were sitting quietly playing a game, I noticed that he still carried God's special mark on his left leg.

Why a story about my grandson? Well, grandfathers have a way of slipping grandchildren stories into all their speaking and writing. But it also serves as a way to start a discussion of God's special birthmarks on His church. Here we are not concerned with the whole church of Jesus Christ, but with your church.

The church you love and care for, perhaps for years, is unique and special. What are some of its special birthmarks. We advise to you compile your own self-image birthmarks. The following list is a sample on how to start.

1. A Spirit of Confidence

Wherever you are—in malls, airports, or on a street corner—you notice people with physical traits that catch your attention. A local church is like that. Every congregation is unique and distinctive from every other church. No other church in the whole world is exactly like yours. The reason: no other church has the same group of people, the same mission, the same setting, the same history, or the same future.

Have you ever thought about how some churches capture the attention of a community more than others? One trait that causes that is a spirit of confidence. It may take many forms—the pastor, a mission program, a church's interest in teens, or a senior citizens emphasis. The forms are nearly endless, but something stands out in the strong church. You may not recognize the personality or you may not like it, but the church, nevertheless, projects a sense of confidence and determination and awareness of mission.

We often wonder what the whole church of Christ would be like if every group of believers were so dedicated to their work that they assumed a position of confidence that shows they believe "the battle is the Lord's" (1 Sam. 17:47), that "if God is for us, who can be against us?" (Rom. 8:31) If we believed with full confidence in Christ, and what He wants us to do, we could easily defeat every enemy.

A similar principle applies in many walks of life. Think about how many successful athletes are actually no more talented than an average player, but they are so motivated by a confident attitude that no one can stop them. They appear to be stronger and to have greater talent than their competitors, but the real difference is confidence. They believe it can be done, and they do it.

We want your church to have confidence like that. You are a winner! Christ has paid the price. He has made you more than a conqueror. Hold your head high. Believe in the One who sent you. Believe in His ability to sustain you. He made you a partner with Omnipotence. Take courage. Go for it. Don't be timid or terrorized. God empowers the spiritually courageous. Remember those strengthening words Paul wrote in Philippians 4:13, "I can do everything through Him who gives me strength." Believe that promise—it is as dependable as the law of gravity. Trust the Lord Jesus to give you confidence in your assignment.

2. A Willingness to Risk

For a church to take a risk means it must be willing to allow the Holy Spirit to push a congregation outside its comfort zone. Try new things. Be open to positive change even if it is frightening. Seek to win new population groups. Take the Gospel to unlikely prospects.

Unless a church attempts something magnificently risky for Christ, it stands still and never invades the enemy's stronghold or succeeds in tearing down the barriers.

One of the great contemporary preachers is East Indian evangelist Samuel T. Kamaleson, who once served as a vice president at World Vision. In a letter to H.B., he talks of the risks Caleb took throughout his life. You remember, Caleb willingly risked so he might inhabit the Promised Land. But even as an old man, he longed for an opportunity to rout the pagan enemy. Dr. Sam wrote these inspiring words of faith:

> Caleb returned from scouting Palestine to say that God would enable the children of Israel to overcome the giants who possessed the land. Years later, when Moses was parceling out the land to the tribes, Caleb, now eighty-five and still confident of God's sustaining power, claimed the territory where he had seen the giants. Caleb said, "Now give me this hill country that the Lord promised me that day. You yourself heard then that the Anakites were there and their cities were large and fortified, but, the Lord helping me, I will drive them out just as He said" (Josh. 14:12).

Willingness to take risks has little to do with age but a lot to do with faith and trust.

A congregation who believes in God and themselves will take risks like Caleb did. In the process, risk-taking translates into full dependence on God. Following their victories, a congregation will have a growing positive and realistic self-image. Like Caleb, their persistence and commitment will be contagious. Over time, the whole atmosphere of the church changes for the better.

3. A Willingness to Resolve Differences

It was a moment in American history that many people missed. Remember the incident in Los Angeles when Rodney King was brutally beaten by the police? The video of that spectacle was seen the world over on TV. It caused outrage among the black and white communities. The ramifications of the trial were monumental. But during the tempestuous proceedings, Rodney King simply asked, "Can't we all just get along?" That comment has echoed in many places in our society, and it must be heard in the church. "Can't we all just get along?"

A church that believes in itself and has a healthy self-image finds happy ways to resolve differences because it believes every person has value. Such a church firmly believes no one has all the answers or the only answer. As a result, people listen to one another. Before issues cause misunderstandings, one person puts aside his wishes for the will of the whole. Power bases are dismantled, and listening posts are established. Decisions are made to improve a church's ability to fulfill its mission. People genuinely care for one another. What an impression that makes on outsiders, and how proud it must make our Heavenly Father.

4. A Willingness to Share

A sharing church has a benevolent spirit, which means it takes pleasure in making life more bearable for others. We have yet to see a church, regardless of size, with an "others first" mind set that did not feel good about itself. It takes positive pride in what God has allowed it to do. And its generosity encourages other churches to do the same.

One of the little-known, rarely mentioned characteristics of Focus on the Family is its willingness to respond to the needs of those who seek help. The Colorado Springs-based ministry is sometimes taken advantage of, but its determination to serve those who have needs is not tainted by the negative. God has blessed Dr. James Dobson and Focus on the Family beyond description. Perhaps that blessing has a lot to do with Focus on the Family's desire to put the needs of others first.

The church that finds ways to use its resources and talents for the advancement of the Gospel and for the betterment of humankind will always feel good about itself. We remember the feeling in churches we pastored that permeated the whole congregation when we reached a goal that allowed us to build a church somewhere in the world, or assist an inner-city ministry, or provide food for the needy in our community.

Such a positive feeling is difficult to explain, but let's try it. In counseling, a minister sometimes works with a stingy father, a leader of the household who will not give freely to the family. Members of the family end up begging, sometimes even being dishonest to get what they need or want. Anger is ever present in the home, and love is almost never communicated. The reason for all of this is that the money handling is out of balance.

The same thing happens when church leaders are stingy with God's money. Sometimes they are not only tightfisted with outside/outreach ministries, but they will not spend money on the church's needs. It results in anger and sometimes disdain for the leaders. A rule of thumb that works well in most churches is this: Take care of your needs, but concentrate your resources on winning the lost, feeding the hungry, and caring for the needy in body, soul, and circumstance.

5. A Willingness to Clearly Define Priorities

All of us become like what we value, because that is where we concentrate our time and energy. The church with a healthy self-image can be identified by its strong interests in Gospel priorities. It does not take newcomers long to see what a church values above all else.

How about your values and your church? Let's consider personal priorities first. They show in what we talk about. Our conversation gives us away. They show in the pictures we display in our home and carry in our wallet. They show in the way we spend money. The Bible says our heart will be set on our treasure. We give to organizations we believe in and want to see prosper. We spend money on things that make us happy.

Another important indicator of our values are friends we hold dear. It takes time and effort, sometimes even sacrifice, to be a good friend. Our thought life is another indication of what we value in life. "As [a man] thinketh in his heart" is the way the Bible puts it (Prov. 23:7).

You don't have to be around an individual long until you can accurately identify the things that make his existence meaningful.

Use this same evaluation for your church. What kind of image does your church family have? How does the church want others to think of your congregation?

Creating a Healthy Congregational Self-Image

So many churches have settled for so much less than they could have and do. They have caved into pressures from the world and basically said, "We can't fight." Meanwhile, other congregations face the challenges of the enemy head-on. Though they do not win every battle, they refuse to be passive. They fight to be conquerors. And they succeed so many more times than their passive neighbors.

A Checklist for Creating a Strong Self-Image

There are several positive steps you can take to improve your church's self-image immediately. These corrections will blunt existing negative forces and help your congregation become a strongly effective part of the conquering church, against whom Jesus promised "the gates of hell shall not prevail" (Matt. 16:18, KJV).

See Your Church As Important to God and Society

Refuse to allow Satan or anyone in or out of your church to make you feel inferior. Look realistically at your church—remember who is the Captain of the ship. Check out what is taking place. If you find areas of ministry with less quality than our Lord deserves, improve them. Hold your head up. Rejoice in the fact that your church is special. And remember the church is needed now more than ever before in human history.

Believe God has something important for your church to accomplish for Him now. When you recall that Christ said He would build His church in spite of every difficulty, the thermometer of your spirit will rise, and folks around you will recognize you deeply love the Savior. Then your service for Christ through the church will be a joyful adventure. Determine to move forward at any cost. It is God's will that the church always advance.

Resist Traditional Ruts

Folk wisdom is right when it says a rut can become a grave if you don't keep moving. To serve this present age—our calling—every church must try new methods and implement innovative strategies for impacting the future. There need be no contradiction between new methods and the timeless message. In her finest hour throughout

167

human history, the church has been quick to try new methodologies while continuing to preach the changeless Gospel.

Remember, every traditional practice was once an innovation someone probably said would not work. There is no spiritual merit in continuing to do things the old way. Often sameness simply means we are sloppy in our planning or dull in our thinking. A church that does everything the same over time becomes oblivious to the environment and people around it. Some new strategy or worship improvement is needed right now at the center of your congregation's life. Drop your fear of change by realizing that the average person is not as opposed to innovation as many church leaders think, for the simple reason that all of us face innovation every day.

Don't Get Used to Sin and Evil
Sin and evil destroy all that is good in the human experience. It's frighteningly easy to get used to the dark. Don't forget we have an enemy who hates our mission and will defeat us if he can. No church can be satisfied to rest on past blessings or yesterday's spiritual achievements. A church's self-image is always raised when it remembers it is in a battle for righteousness against the enemy of our soul.

Fan the Flame of Urgency
Our God-given mission is to win our neighbors and a dying world. A sense of urgency is needed. With morality declining all around us and church attendance shrinking, it's time to rise up and be about the mission of Christ in the world. It's time to pray and act with urgency when we see families fractured by marital conflict, when adultery is wrecking so many homes, when apathy is so prevalent, and when the church has become worldly.

Intercession is needed. Diligence is required. Persistence is demanded. Devotion to the Gospel is needed. A holy ruggedness is required. As Southern evangelist-statesman Vance Havner wrote years ago:

A real Christian is a rugged, sturdy soul who is under no illusions about life and is grappling with things as they are. He is not always agreeable and sweet, for he must be uncompromising and firm amidst a superficial world. He is no lamb-like creature forever mumbling prayers and universally pleasant. He is a battle-scarred warrior who does not confuse singing an anthem with fighting the good fight.

Then, Havner calls for holy urgency: "Being a Christian means being husky for heaven's sake and rugged for righteousness' sake. Better be out in the scrimmage and make a thousand errors than sit on the sidelines in blissful piety and never risk your idealism in the clash with reality."[1]

Renew Respect for the Appearance of Facilities

Take pride in the facilities you have. Make them as attractive as possible. A coat of paint can make a big difference. Clean windows, throw away hand-me-downs. A little hard work makes things look much better. Make your church buildings say, "Somebody loves this place." Take a realistic look at the wear and tear on your facilities and do whatever it takes to make the house of God attractive, even beautiful.

Keep an Outreach Focus

If you were a new person seeking a church home or an unbeliever seeking Christ, would it be easy to find a happy entrance to the fellowship of your church? Try looking at all you do through the eyes of persons who attend for the first time.

Too many churches lock the world out by saying unintentionally, "We are satisfied with who we are and what we have." We must be like Christ. We must open our hearts to anyone who needs love and acceptance. Please don't let your church be comfortable with "just the family" in ministry.

Value Your Pastor

This subject has been discussed on nearly every page of this book, so it is only necessary here to note that a healthy congregational self-image is affected by the love and concern a congregation shows for its minister. Often pastoral relationship is a microcosm of the way persons in the congregation treat each other. A congregation that respects and cares for its spiritual leader feels good about itself. On the contrary, a church that takes advantage of its shepherd feels guilty and small. Laypeople need to be sentries on constant lookout for anything that might invalidate the effectiveness of their pastor or send a signal to a watching world that they have carelessly treated God's anointed leader.

Remember Ownership

Never forget your church belongs to Christ. Charles Colson summarizes this issue well when he reminds us:

> The church is not a democracy and never can be. We can change rules and practices and sing new hymns and use different styles of worship. We can change forms, but not our foundations. For the church is authoritarian. It is ruled over by Christ the Head and governed by a constitution that cannot be ignored or amended.[2]

All of us who try to lead the church in any way can chuckle in agreement with Hilaire Belloc's remark as reported by Malcolm Muggeridge: "The church must be in God's hands because, seeing the people who have run it, it couldn't possibly have gone on existing if there weren't some help from above."[3] Rejoice in the reality that the church is the personal possession of Christ.

How Would You Rate Your Church?

Now that we have walked through these simple though significant ideas about improving your church's self-concept, how would you rate your congregation? Remember, your answers indicate whether or not your church is effective and alive or just "another church" in a town or city of many other churches.

We urge you, as a pillar of your congregation, to sit down with other church leaders and use these helps for building a strong congregational self-image to evaluate your congregation. If you pass the evaluation with flying colors, cheer your church. If improvements are needed, get started now. So much depends on decisive action to move ahead.

Creating a Healthy Congregational Self-Image

In Exodus 14, the children of Israel were in a sense of disarray. Moses was downtrodden. They were not feeling good about themselves. At that time God stepped in and commanded Moses to "move on." And Moses said to the people, "Do not be afraid. Stand firm and you will see the deliverance the Lord will bring you today. . . . The Lord will fight for you!" (vv. 13-14)

We urge you to go forward. When it's dark, look for the light. When it's daytime, look for the cloud of promise. The Lord God is with you. He offers all the power at His command, and that is more than you need.

Consider this incredible insight from former United States Senate Chaplain Richard Halverson: "The church that Christ is building confronts the world, not by cleverness or wisdom, not by programs or methods or institutions. The church Christ is building confronts the world in the very power of God himself in the life of the believers. The Chaplain is right—our strength is in God."[4]

It's an awesome truth—building great churches means building great Christians. That makes every church a gathering place of eternally and spiritually significant people. That gives every congregation everlasting relevance. That makes every believer a "somebody" of inestimable value. What a strong self-image this truth creates for every congregation in every setting around the world. You're in the middle of the action.

RENEWAL STRATEGIES FOR CHURCH PILLARS
How to Keep Your Church Holy and Healthy

1. Be comfortable with what God wants the church to be.

2. Correct causes of low self-image: location, reputation, purpose, and leadership.

3. Celebrate your church's distinctives.

4. Build congregational confidence.

5. Risk taking the Gospel to the cutting edge of society.

6. Find happy ways to resolve differences.

7. Take care of your congregation's financial needs but concentrate a wholesome generosity on others.

8. Define and convey your congregation's priorities.

9. Remind decision makers that every tradition was once an innovative idea.

10. Emphasize who really owns the church.

"For the church is not a human society of people united by their natural affinities but the body of Christ, in which all members, however different, must share the common life, complementing and helping one another precisely by their differences."

C.S. Lewis

9. A PASTOR'S BILL OF RIGHTS

Liberating Your Minister to Greatness

Holy God—the One who calls and sustains our minister—
    show us how to better encourage our pastor,
    to love our pastor better
    to challenge our pastor to greatness,
    to follow our pastor, where You lead,
    to affirm our pastor's strengths, and
    to pray for our pastor.
        Keep our pastor from becoming an endangered species. Amen.

Pastors' rights. What? Never heard of such a thing? What would a bill of rights say? Why is it necessary? And what will it accomplish?

Consider what a bill of rights is supposed to do. Check any encyclopedia to learn details such as James Madison led in formulating the document, for the purpose of ensuring ratification of the United States Constitution by the states. Concepts found in the Bill of Rights are deeply rooted in the Bible and in Greek and Roman civilizations. Historical personalities like John Locke, John Milton, John Stuart Mill, and Thomas Paine all had a strong part in shaping the U.S. Bill of Rights, which went into effect in 1791. The Bill of Rights has protected Americans' fundamental liberties for more than 200 years. Similar documents guarantee rights in Great Britain, France, Canada, and the United Nations.

175

Your Pastor Is an Endangered Species

When a pastoral bill of rights is suggested, several concerns come to mind immediately. Rights, on the most basic level, require responsible relationships between two or more parties. That's an important part of this whole picture. For example, civil rights guarantee protection for citizens. Children's rights prescribe responsibilities by home and government to children. Patients' rights charge physicians, medical staff, insurance providers, and hospitals to have responsibility to sick people. In Western civilizations, workers' rights ensure employees a right to be paid, to be provided with adequate tools, and to have a safe working environment. Rights grow out of responsibilities based on relationships. Thus, responsible relationships between pastors and parishioners is the cornerstone for formulating a pastor's bill of rights.

Laypersons also have rights in church. Everyone understands that lay believers have rights for full acceptance, hearing the Gospel, faithful ministry from a pastor, and an opportunity of fulfilling service. They have family rights because they were adopted into God's family at the time of their conversion. These rights are based on Scripture, redemptive relationships, standard practices throughout church history, and previous experiences in a particular congregation.

Rights between a pastor and a congregation, however, are unique among all human associations. These rights are not like those between employer and employee. These rights are different from a pay-for-service relationship such as doctors or lawyers have with patients or clients. Neither are pastoral rights a legal guaranteed right, such as equal opportunity, airline safety, or clean water. Consequently, because a pastor's rights are unique, they are sometimes forgotten or ignored.

Let's discuss those rights so we can understand them and make full use of them. What obligations does a congregation owe a pastor? What rights should every congregation give a pastor? What entitlements go with a call to ministry? Closely connected to these concerns is an even more important question—can a congregation be an authentic church without granting rights of leadership to its pastor?

This book has been written to build bridges of relationships between church pillars and clergy. For churches that already possess wholesome connections with their pastors, we have tried to fortify and encourage and celebrate those relationships. For others, we have suggested ways to circumvent problems before they start. For other congregations experiencing difficulties, we have offered strategies for restoration and renewal.

In summary form we want to restate the key issues in a pastor's bill of rights; many of these ideas are a restatement of earlier ideas sprinkled throughout this book. Though John D. Rockefeller probably did not have churches in mind, his advice applies with incredible accuracy: "Every right implies a responsibility; every opportunity, an obligation; every possession, a duty."[1]

I. The Right to Dream

As a young pastor, H.B. remembers sharing his dreams with his first congregation. Like many churches, the congregation had several lay leaders who seemed determined to sabotage his vision. Try to see the picture clearly. It was his first church. He was young with a new seminary degree in his hand. His dreams were simple but significant visions of what he believed God could do in his first assignment.

Sadly, a small group of experienced foot draggers stymied H.B.'s dreams. No one wanted to challenge these power brokers because of their contentious spirit. As often happens, these controllers were neither spiritually minded nor forward thinking. Rather, they were self-centered people who wanted control so they could have prominence. Controllers usually want to rule or ruin. These leaders wanted to keep everything as it was so they could be in charge; they were rashly wrong in seeking to keep the church in a status quo mode.

An important warning should be sounded and heeded. Laypersons must be aware of the possible consequences before they allow themselves to get stuck in this quagmire. God judges those who sabotage the work of the congregation. Though it may be a hard lesson for those addicted to power, the church is no plaything. The church is an eternal vine of the Lord's planting—the body of Christ, the family of God, the people of God. The church is God's instrument for saving a lost world. Therefore, those who turn a church into a social power base defile Christ's mission for His church. Those who thwart God's purpose stand in judgment. Let controllers everywhere carefully consider the serious repercussions before they thwart a God-given dream of an anointed leader.

That is exactly what happened in the church H.B. served. New people attended. Lives were transformed. Human miracles of God's grace, however, were not impressed by the power brokers' base but by what God was doing in their lives. The congregation was like those standing on the edge of Jesus' ministry as He worked miracles. Some were in the crowd because of their spiritual struggles and hungers. Others came looking for opportunities to shut down the Gospel any way they could. However, the spiritual groundswell was so infectious for a period of time that power-hungry folks could not stop it. But they kept alert to every possible opportunity. They tried to kill the dream by crucifying the leader. But they misjudged because the dream lived on.

A similar thing happens today. As a pastor shares God-given dreams, congregations begin seeing their church in a whole new way. Then a crisis starts. As the Lord walks in the midst of His church, power controllers stand in the shadows, undercutting the value of the progress. In many cases, the pastor can't survive because controllers see to it that any advance seems too difficult or too expensive—even when it's not.

Think of the incredible losses that follow. Those who have been considering accepting Christ give up to leave the church to those who want it, like a childish game of marbles on the school playground. Dreamers stop dreaming or they become reluctant to share new dreams. Potential believers lose interest, sometimes for a lifetime. Pastors move. Controllers shrivel up spiritually because they know they have wrecked the potential of their church. In the process, power brokers often lose their children and grandchildren to the faith. Meanwhile, these same controllers suspect every church that is showing progress and winning new people.

Dreams are fragile. Before you criticize another person's dream, remember this wisdom from an unknown sage: "It [a dream] can be killed by a sneer or a yawn; it can be stabbed to death by a quip and worried to death by a frown on the right person's brow."[2] That's serious stuff.

Here's a self-test to help you determine if you are a champion or killer of dreams.

178

- Do you encourage your pastor to dream?
- Are you a help or hindrance to your pastor's dream?
- Are you an affirmer or a foot dragger?
- Do you ask "why not" or "how come" when you hear a dream for your church?
- Do you pray that your pastor will be uniquely blessed with creative ways to touch people?
- Do you tell your pastor, "Go for it!" or do you ride the spiritual bus with your foot on the brake?

The positive thinker Norman Vincent Peale challenged church leaders to "be a possibilitarian. No matter how dark things seem to be or actually are, raise your sights and see possibilities—always see them, for they're always there." That's what your pastor needs from you. Not all dreams will work, but some will. Fruitful dreams will broaden your church's ministry and grow your pastor's soul. Meanwhile, you will find joy in becoming a dream cheerleader and your faith in what God can do will flourish.

II. The Right to Privacy

Compassion and availability make a pastor live in a glass house where the work is never finished and where the welcome is expected to be warm at all times. For some inexplicable reason, churches—especially smaller fellowships—sometimes behave as if they own the pastor and his family.

Think of the intrusive situations you have heard of or perhaps caused. Church pillars pry into a pastor's family matters. Board members question how a minister spends his money. One snoopy busybody pieced together bits of a torn-up letter from a pastor's wastebasket and started rumors. One congregation thought its pastor dressed too expensively, and the next church called her dreadfully plain. Some criticize the minister's car—it's too new, too old, too red, or too expensive. Some churches expect a minister's children will never act like children. It's a strange world where the "privacy please" sign is seldom observed.

Responsible lay leaders should do all they can to respect the privacy of the pastoral family and encourage others to do the same. When a young pastor's wife wore a maternity dress for the first time, a gossiper remarked to a lay leader, "Well, it's about time. They've been married five years." The lay leader responded quietly, "They have as much right to privacy as you do." The reply quieted the gossiper for a few minutes, or perhaps for a few hours. But probably not for long.

Since the nature of ministry makes a pastor live in a glass house, allow him opportunity to pull down the shades and shut the world out just like other people do. Allow your minister an occasional time of family togetherness, marriage privacy, and isolated hours for digging into the deepest realities of godliness. A German proverb shines light on the need for privacy between a pastor and his congregation: "A hedge between keeps friendships green." The hedge is a respect for privacy. A great pastor lives continually with a near-equal combination of availability and privacy. Both should be respected and honored.

How does privacy look for a pastor? It is often nothing more than the simple satisfactions everyone else enjoys in everyday living. Privacy means uninterrupted meals, time with family members, time to stare into space, time to watch TV, time to pray, time to sit on the front stoop with a child and watch the world go by, or time to recover from Sunday's strains. With an apology to former Archbishop of Canterbury Geoffrey Fisher for taking some editorial license, "There is a sacred realm of privacy for every pastor where he makes his own choices and decisions—a place of his own essential rights and liberties into which the church, generally speaking, must not intrude."[3] Fisher is right. Every minister needs a space where the church does not intrude. Give your pastor privacy as part of helping him be a fulfilled human being.

Urge your pastor to let the congregation know his family mealtimes, what his day off is, and when his family has devotional times together. Since many pastors might be reticent about announcing such preferences, lay leaders can share this information during pastor appreciation events, or it could be printed in Sunday bulletins or weekly newsletters as communication from lay leaders. Help fellow church persons understand that a pastor's home and study is where a minister goes to recoup, pray, study, think, unwind, and gain perspective—a place for refueling before going among the people again.

The essence of a pastor's work means that an evening or weekend to regroup is seldom available. Saturday and Sunday are a pastor's busy time to be with people and lead the church in worship—a weekend off almost never happens. Surveys show pastors average less than two nights per week at home. Consequently, family time is always at a premium.

For these reasons, concerned lay leaders should sometimes question a pastor about how much time is spent with spouse and children. Encourage your minister to spend quality time with the most important people in her life. Help your pastor protect limited privacy. Lead a charge to help your pastor take more time away from the church. Time away doesn't cost—it pays. A well-rested pastor with a balanced schedule always serves a church better over the long haul and will be a more well-rounded person.

Ask these questions as part of the continuing self-test:

• Do you or the decision group make unreasonable demands on your pastor?

• Do you take liberties with a minister's living quarters?

• Do you stand firm for the pastor's family when others question lifestyle issues?

• Do you ask your pastor tough accountability questions regarding schedule and quality time with family?

III. The Right to Adequate Income

As an old joke goes, a layman once prayed, "Lord, You keep the pastor humble and we'll keep him poor." Though this may not have actually happened, it nearly always causes a nervous chuckle because it contains a measure of truth. As everyone knows, pastors are seldom paid enough. The sad reality is many churches could pay better with a little extra effort, but they don't try. Few churches ever have felt squeezed economically for giving a generous raise to their pastor.

It is no secret that a pastor, or spouse, is often forced by economic necessity to be employed in the secular workplace so he can stay in the ministry. Let that fact sink in. Because of limited income, many ministers' spouses feel responsible to furnish economic safety nets that keep the minister in the service of the church.

Such sacrifice should be cherished and never wasted. Laypeople must take the lead to see their pastor is appropriately compensated. Ministerial support is every congregation's first financial obligation. No pastor should have to move to another church for financial reasons, but it happens somewhere every week. Though other reasons for leaving are politely given, some ministers have been "starved out." That sometimes means controllers withhold their giving to force a pastor's resignation.

Surveys show the average pastor needs an immediate annual increase of $2,000 to $8,000. Contrary to what some people think, money matters for ministers are not mysterious or hard to understand. Church decision groups sometimes act as if they don't understand costs of inflation, auto operations, sports shoes for teenagers, college tuition, professional books, and respectable clothing. Like every other family, there has to be enough money to meet the needs.

One of the things lay leaders can do is to consider ways to help lessen a minister's "worry factor." Few pastors are in ministry for financial gain. Most feel called by God. At a life-changing crossroad, they answered a call from God to the Christian ministry, knowing there would be sacrifices. This commitment is like "for better or worse" in marriage. Though pastors do not often complain about money, they need lots of help with the worry factor. As you might expect, they worry about whether things will ever be different financially. They worry about college bills for the children and retirement costs.

Lay leaders can help decrease the worry factor by simply asking a minister occasionally, "Pastor, how are you doing financially?" Then listen and do something about it. If you don't ask the question, who will? And if you don't follow through on possible solutions, how will the situation ever improve?

Here are some more self-test questions for church pillars:

• Do you know the average compensation of pastors in your community? Rejoice if your church pays more and take action if your church pays less.

• Do you know if your pastor has outstanding debt on tuition bills from Bible college or seminary? Why not lead your church to help underwrite a portion of those expenses as long as your pastor serves your congregation?

• Does your decision group review your pastor's compensation twice each year? In that review, be sure to consider car allowance, retirement benefits, salary raises, social security insurance, and health and dental insurance in your decisions.

• Do you regularly consider the pastor's housing? If the church owns a parsonage, maintenance costs should be built into the budget. A congregation can take as much pride in their pastor's housing as they take in their church facilities or their own homes.

IV. The Right to Continual Professional Development

Ministry, unlike other professions, is self-directed. A pastor lives with his own ideas, hears his own voice, and serves the same people week after week. The physician is different because he or she consults with colleagues on a daily basis at the hospital; some are involved in partnership practices, so they have constant contact with others in their profession. Lawyers often work in combined law practices and have frequent conversations with accountants, physicians, judges, and civic authorities. Teachers enjoy daily contact with fellow teachers and principals to help them keep their skills sharp and to test their conclusions. But because most pastors have almost none of these associations, they need opportunities for professional dialogue and continued development.

Many clergy, having been out of Bible college and seminary for years, are frighteningly out of touch with contemporary church trends and changes in society. They are at perilous disadvantage. One pastor wrote recently, "I just don't have what it takes to go with all the changes I see on the horizon of the church. What do I do?"

And this pastor is not alone. Studies show the words "inadequate" and "confused" pop up whenever pastors are asked to describe their ministry—a predictable result of doing ministry in isolation with the same people for an extended time. Such isolation leads to ministerial monotony, professional boredom, and emotional burnout. The result is an unimaginative sameness in ministry.

Everything is changing, including us. Christian researcher George Barna believes our culture redefines itself twice every ten years. That means the surroundings and atmosphere of ministry are significantly different than they have ever been before. As a result, the way we do church keeps changing too. Meanwhile, many pastors do not understand how to change or why innovation is necessary. Many even argue that the church must stay the same since the redemptive work of God is changeless. The trick, of course, is to know the difference between the unchanging message and changing methodologies.

The toughest part of developing an awareness to make these distinctions is that many pastors have no frame of reference or formal training for making needed changes. To help pastors understand their environment and maximize ministry to contemporary people, they need frequent opportunities to update their skills and refresh their concepts. Without these opportunities, the church will probably become increasingly more outdated and less relevant.

Decision groups must make more opportunities available for pastors to better understand their times. But how can it be done? It usually starts by providing money to attend development events, followed by a serious commitment on a minister's part to participate in such events. A generous allowance should be built into a congregation's financial planning so the pastor can attend conferences, take college courses, visit other churches, be involved in overseas mission trips, and read lots of books.

Such funding does cost a church but is an investment in expanded creativity, deepened sensitivity, and a rekindled passion for ministry in contemporary settings. Continual professional development and upgrading of skills helps pastors do their work better, gives an increased sense of achievement, and helps them feel up-to-date in their various expressions of their ministry. Everybody in the church wins when a pastor enjoys personal fulfillment and professional development.

Here are more self-test questions regarding pastoral development lay leaders can ask themselves:

• When was the last time your church made it possible for your pastor to attend a clergy conference for upgrading skills?

• Has your pastor ever thought about pursuing a higher level of education? Has your leadership team encouraged the pastor and offered funds to do so?

• If your church has a professional staff, are they strongly encouraged to attend at least one annual event for professional growth?

• Have you encouraged your clergy couple to attend a marriage enrichment event at least once every two years?

Consider this comparison. Would you want a physician who did not stay current regarding the latest medical advances or newest medications? Would you want a tax consultant who was unaware of the latest tax laws? Would you want your children's teachers to give up their in-service training, an obvious benefit to your child as well as to the teachers? Why not think the same way about ministers as you do other professionals?

Our culture is in confusing change. Habits of church people are changing radically. Therefore, the church must refine its way of doing business in order to reach more contemporary people. No pastor can do that without encouragement and funding to continually update his skills and stir his creativity.

V. The Right of Friendship

To be a well-adjusted human being, everyone needs friends. But have you thought about who your pastor's best friend might be? Is it his spouse? Is it you? Is it another pastor? Is it a person in the community? In all probability, it is none of the above.

The average pastor has few genuinely close friends. Eight out of ten pastors say they have no one to openly interact with about professional and personal concerns other than their spouse. For the majority of pastors, their closest friend is their spouse, but loading too many ministry details on one's mate can overload emotional circuits in the marriage.

Every pastor needs a close friend in addition to their spouse. But a serious problem exists because many ministerial training programs, our tight-lipped culture, and petty rivalries in congregations argue against it. Many seminary professors and highly placed church leaders have warned pastors not to have close friends inside or outside the church. Older colleagues often advise, "Don't trust anyone." Church members sometimes pout if they know their pastor has a close friend in the congregation. The same folks feel threatened if their pastor has friends in the community. Followed to a logical conclusion, all this means pastors are expected to be friendless.

This no-special-friendship idea is wrong and damages a pastor's wholeness. Friends are good for health and refreshing to the spirit. Without them, ministry loses much of its radiance and meaning. In a 1983 commencement address at Cornell University, Frank H.T. Rhodes offered a profound insight about friends that provides an important message to clergy: "Without friendship and the openness and trust that go with it, skills are barren and knowledge may become an unguided missile."[4] Most of us could easily identify pastors who fit that description perfectly.

So for everyone's benefit, encourage your pastor to find a best friend, a confidant. This is a favor you do your church as well as your minister. The success of her ministry likely depends on it.

H.B. received a letter from a pastor's wife who tried to surprise her husband with a birthday party. She had invited several friends from the church, a few people from the community, and an assortment of relatives. The party was fun. The pastor had been having tough times in his work, so it was good to see him laugh. The pastor's wife was uplifted when the party was over, but she was unprepared for what followed. The next Sunday, she and her husband were confronted by several lay leaders who told them in no uncertain terms that "private parties" such as she had planned for her husband were forbidden. They also reminded her that her husband was pastor of the whole church, so she could either invite everyone or stop having parties. The pastor's wife was devastated and angry, with good reason. No minister should be expected to forego personal friendship just because he is a pastor.

The friendships provide obvious benefits like relaxing and laughing and sharing when burdens get heavy. A friend often makes the difference between coping and over-stress. Without friends, a pastor can be suffocated by the loneliness of ministry. Encourage your pastor to have friends inside and outside the church. A pastor, like every human being, can do his work well while at the same time having close friends who are not connected to his profession in any way.

Another advantage of having friends is accountability. Every pastor needs someone to ask hard questions about his marriage, walk with God, ethical and moral standards, parenting, and commitments to ministry. Friends help keep a pastor principled and authentic.

Few people know the pastor's work well enough to ask the right questions at just the right time. Therefore, when your pastor finds someone who is a genuine friend, do not make him feel guilty about the association. Rather, encourage and rejoice about the richness such an association brings to his ministry. An accountability friend will help your pastor serve better and have a closer relationship to God and family.

Try these questions to evaluate your pastor's freedom to cultivate close friendships:

• Are you a potential best friend to your pastor?
• Do you defend your pastor's right to have friends?
• How would your church handle the birthday party mentioned earlier? How would you react if you were not invited to the party?
• How can you encourage your pastor to have a soul friend who will hold him accountable?

VI. The Right for Protection from Unrealistic Scrutiny

Nearly everyone realizes how difficult it is to overlook misdirected words or insensitive acts that hurt one's mate or family. But because ministers live in glass houses, it's easy for a layperson to see a weakness in a spiritual leader. To complicate matters, people love to discuss public persons and their families; that explains the attraction of TV programs like "Lifestyles of the Rich and Famous." When all this is added together, laity should not be surprised when they find their pastor is super-protective of his family. Many ministers find it difficult to tolerate even a hint of criticism against their family.

To keep this scrutiny problem in balance, several suggestions might be worth discussing in your decision group.

• *Never consider a pastor's spouse to be an unpaid assistant.* Unless a package employment agreement was made at the interview stage, a church should not expect a minister's mate to be an unpaid assistant. In reality, the pastor's spouse is a layperson married to a minister. In the years of your pastor's service to your church, the spouse's involvement will likely increase or decrease depending on family needs, outside workload, and health. Try to view the mate's involvement just as you would that of any other volunteer.

• *Let kids be kids.* It is unfair to expect the minister's children to be role models for children in the congregation. And even if you expect it, you won't get it. At nearly every pastor's conference, several ministry couples share the pain they feel because of their children. Much of this distress is rooted in unrealistic expectations of the minister's children, either by the parents or the congregation. A play center for children in Colorado Springs has an imaginative ad that expresses this idea: "A place where kids can be kids." Why not make your church a place where kids can be kids?

Pastor's children, like all children, come into the world human and subject to the same temptations others experience. Allow a minister's children to develop normally. Talk to them like you would any child. Let them know they are loved for themselves and not because of who their parents are. Give them the benefit of the doubt, like you would your own children. Help create a climate in your church where all children and teens find it easy to seek the Savior.

Some of the saddest people in the whole world are grown children of ministers who never had the opportunity to develop their own faith and uniqueness. For a lifetime, they have chased the elusive carrot of emotional and spiritual health without finding it. On the contrary, some of the most well-adjusted people of faith are those who were loved into wholeness by congregations their pastor/parent served during their childhood and adolescence.

As a church pillar, you can help encourage the spiritual and emotional development of a pastor's child. Try loving your minister's children into joyous faith. Since they are often far away from uncles and aunts and grandparents, become their extended family. Give them space to develop their identity. Allowing these children to see Christ in you may be the most important ministry you will ever accomplish. As years pass, you will see the pastor's children prosper in their spiritual development and know you had a significant part in it. That's satisfying to you and pleasing to God.

• *Don't deliver secondhand messages through the pastor's family.* If you have something to say, say it directly to the pastor. Do not expect the spouse or children to deliver messages. Speak to the pastor yourself so the message will be clear and you will not injure the person you expect to deliver your message. No one has a right to cause a child to ask, "Dad, how come Mr. Smith is angry with you?" Or, "Mom, why are the ladies all talking about your new dress?" Or, "Dad, parents of my church friends don't think you work enough. Why would they say something like that?" Good question—why would they say that?

Christian brothers and sisters must nobly live above such foolishness. The potential damage to a child is too great for anyone to take part in such irrationality. If you want to sour children on the church or undermine their confidence in the family of God, just carelessly criticize their parents. Who wants responsibility for creating such difficult problems? On the contrary, pastors' kids beam with pride when you brag to them about their parents.

Try answering these questions as a self-test:
• When was the last time you let your minister's children know they were cherished?
• Do you praise the minister's children?
• When your pastor's kids act like kids, what do you say to their parents?
• Do you pray for your pastor's children?

VII. The Right to Fail

Jesus was the only perfect person in human history. He never failed. He never sinned. His character always radiated love and goodness. He is our pattern and example. Our Lord was the only one who ever walked on water, though a few of His followers have tried without success.

Pastors are never perfect reproductions of their Lord. Don't expect it and you will not be disappointed. Neither do pastors intentionally fail. No minister purposely wants to disillusion you or hinder the church. The nature of ministry is to give one's life to helping others find joy in being a Christian. Consequently, your pastor never wants to preach a poorly prepared sermon or give wrong counsel. If pastors had their way, they would never miss an appointment or make a bad decision. And if they could, they would walk on water for you. But they can't. Regrettably, they sometimes fail.

In a congregation of senior citizens, Baby Boomers, Busters, power brokers, and adolescents, no human being can keep everyone satisfied all the time. Consequently, pastors must do their best and congregations must accept their best as being good enough. Unfortunately, the best is not good enough for some church members. Those who study forced pastoral terminations believe such action is frequently due to the unwillingness of seven or fewer people to reconcile a difference.

Can you believe it? Seven or fewer unforgiving persons are allowed by the majority to force a pastor's termination. Even though Jesus taught forgiveness throughout Scripture, a small group of unforgiving church persons can determine a pastor's future and create a perilous crisis in the congregation.

There is a better way. Try following the counsel of Jesus in Matthew 18:15: "If your brother sins against you, go and show him his fault, just between the two of you. If he listens to you, you have won your brother over."

Lest anyone think we are trying to defend incompetence or laziness, let's make it clear—we do not think pastors are perfect. Nor do we believe all pastors are sincerely authentic. Some are ill-prepared for their assignment, and some would be better off in secular work. Yet it is dangerously unfair for a small group to determine the future ministry of a pastor. Surely the guidance of God must be sought. To harm those whom God has called to the ministry and anointed for service is a serious deed that produces consequences that will thunder into the future of a church. Whatever the cause of a pastor's termination, painful consequences ricochet in every direction for years.

I (H.B.) once blew it big time in a church I served. No one could have felt worse about my failure than I did. My error was serious enough that it could have undermined the faith of the family I had wronged. They could have made life miserable for me throughout the congregation. I dreaded the confrontation, but it had to come. I sat defenseless in front of a brokenhearted family. I asked them to forgive me. They forgave me and treated me as God treats everyone, as though I had done no wrong. I became a better pastor. God was glorified by forgiveness given and forgiveness received.

Could that happen every time there is a misunderstanding between minister and parishioner? Probably not. Should an attempt be made to resolve every conflict? Every time. Because that is what God expects. He wants it for the spiritual development it causes in all persons involved.

Though not known as a person of faith, Theodore Roosevelt believed in the right to fail and start again. He loved to say,

> It is not the critic who counts, nor the man who points out how the strong man stumbled or where the doer of deeds could have done better. The credit belongs to the man who is actually in the arena, whose face is marred by the dust and sweat and blood; who strives valiantly; who errs and comes up short again and again; who knows the great enthusiasms, the great devotions, and spends himself in a worthy cause; who, at the best, knows in the end the triumph of high achievement; and who at the worst, if he fails, at least fails while daring greatly, so that his place shall never be with those cold and timid souls who know neither victory nor defeat.[5]

What an encouragement these words are to every pastor who has tried and failed. It's time to try again, and it's time for church pillars to give a pastor another opportunity for effective ministry.

VIII. The Right of Passage

From several studies and continuing dialogue with ministers, we conclude that as many as one in four pastors has experienced at least one forced termination in the years of their service.

How does that happen? Depending on the church's governance, a congregation can vote "no confidence" or a decision board can vote to terminate the pastoral relationship. Another more common, though unofficial, way is for a disgruntled group to work cunningly against the pastor, making it so difficult to do effective ministry that the minister chooses to leave. Another devilish technique is to start false rumors that have no basis in fact. Sadly, when such undercurrents start, there is almost no way to stop them, and in time the pastor's ministry is damaged beyond repair. Ministry usually ends when credibility is destroyed.

A pastor friend suffered through six years of contention in his congregation. The church grew. People's lives were transformed. A new building was erected. An overwhelmingly positive congregational vote gave our friend and family the right to stay. But they finally gave up and moved.

Like a dripping faucet in the background of church life, there were damaging accusations and mixed messages from a small group of disgruntled people. Finally, the pastor and his family could no longer tolerate the opposition either emotionally or spiritually. They left. The pastor's future ministry had been damaged and the potential of the church had been sabotaged by the selfish aims of a few. They simply wore the pastor down. It's not right. It shouldn't happen. But it is happening right now even as you read these words.

Consider the dreadful fallout of forced terminations. In the process, a church is usually held hostage by those who seize control. Potential converts think the church is a counterfeit absurdity. Disgruntled folks, when they try to pray, know who caused the havoc and who bears responsibility in God's judgment. Ministers' families are spiritually scarred forever. Even neighboring pastors who are not terminated feel stifled by what happens to colleagues, so morale plummets in their churches. As a result, the voice of the prophet is stilled and the challenging demands of the Gospel are neglected in places well beyond the local congregation. Some ministers quit permanently; others develop a lifelong distrust of church members. Predictably, the church gets a bad name in the community, so the authenticity of the Gospel is doubted across a community for years to come. The final blow comes when solid members get tired of the sham and move on to another church, leaving the congregation in control of those who provoked the problem. When this sabotage is complete, the congregation calls another pastor. Then the process starts over again because the controllers have outwitted and outlasted the spiritually sound folks.

So the tragedy continues. Some churches are on their third or fourth time of such destructive foolishness. Busy spending big dollars on candidating and moving a new pastor, members of dysfunctional congregations know they will face the same difficulties again in a few months or years because nothing has changed except a former pastor moved.

It's time to ask some serious questions and take drastic action. Healing prescriptions or painful surgeries are needed. Someone must champion intercession and revival.

Of course, the reverse side of long pastorates also must be considered. Ministers should not stay forever. Churches sometimes outgrow pastors, and pastors sometimes outgrow churches. That's life. If a transition seems to be in the will of God, then let it be done with grace and magnanimity.

A line from Kenny Roger's earthy country song highlights a more spiritual lesson: "You have to know when to hold them and know when to fold them." The analogy for a congregation is this—there is far too much transition on every level of church life, including the moving of pastors and the migration of church members. Moving, as bad as it is, seems better than facing and solving issues that divide us. Kingdom efforts are often weakened because we are quick-change artists. There is a time to move and a time to stay the course. In many settings, more spiritually minded lay leaders are desperately needed who count the high costs of changing pastors and determine that improving an existing pastoral relationship may be much better than establishing a new one.

IX. The Right to Organizational Support

The value and difficulties of denominations and associations of churches have been debated during most of this century and will likely be debated well into the next century. We have no intention of fueling more controversy on these well-discussed issues. It appears that churches and pastors serve in denominational organizations to provide stability and direction for doctrinal issues, church colleges, efficiency and continuity of missionary ministries, church planting, and care of the clergy. Those issues are of obvious importance in both denominational and independent churches.

But clergy-in-crisis has become an urgent new dilemma facing all churches. This issue is bearing down on contemporary churches like a thirty-two-wheeler speeding out of control down a mountain pass. This crisis has shown up in staggering proportions in all church groups, from Pentecostal to Catholic and every group in between. What was formerly ignored for so long is finally being faced. What was denied did not go away. Issues many people chose to overlook are now pushing the church to action. Since these changes are taking place so quickly, denominational agencies are shocked and experiencing great difficulty in determining how to prioritize redemptive responses to the problem.

This crisis must be solved if the church is to have a viable future in many places. A church cannot be the church God wants without pastors who are holy and whole. Trashing clergy by systems, power brokers, or even pastors themselves cannot go on much longer without the church passing a point of no return. No army can fight with over-stressed, hungry, depressed, crippled soldiers. No army can expect to win a war when its warriors are under attack from the front by the enemy and from the rear by its own troops. No army can fight when army headquarters puts more resources into foreign aid than into defense. Yet that is exactly what the army of the Lord does in many places.

The Lord's army must have its troops in the best spiritual, physical, and emotional fighting condition possible. Anything less means more soldiers will be wounded or killed in the line of fire. It also means more casualties, more deserters, more wounded, more morale problems, and more Purple Hearts will be deserved.

To stimulate a more effective response to these problems, consider the following suggestions of how a denomination or association of churches can support pastors and local churches. Meanwhile, let's face the reality that these groups are made up of individuals like us, so we may need to take the first steps in response strategies. Thus, these suggestions are as much for us to implement as for anyone else.

1. Affirmation. Affirm a minister's importance as a member of the pastoral team. The attitude should be, "How can our association of churches or our denomination enable the called, anointed servant of the church to do front-line ministry?"

2. Safety. Provide a safe haven for those going through emotional, relational, spiritual, or physical challenges. This should be done for the sake of the pastor, for the family, and to insure future usefulness to the cause of Christ. Someone has to nurse the wounded back to vibrant health.

3. Pastoral Care. Develop a pastor for pastors. This person should have no administrative or credentialing authority over ministers. However caring ecclesiastical leaders may be, it is difficult for a pastor to discuss personal issues with one who has authority over future placement.

4. Team Building. Seek regular input from pastors about programs, methods, and expenditures of the larger body to nourish a sense of belonging.

5. Development. Provide annual, quality, and relevant personal and spiritual development opportunities for pastors. Encourage larger churches to give scholarships to ministers serving churches with limited financial resources.

6. Benefits. Establish a plan of minimum compensation and insurance benefits for pastoral families. Such benefits could be classified as full support or bi-vocational. No church should expect to have a full-time pastor when it does not pay a minimum full-time salary. Neither should a pastor with small pastoral responsibilities serving in a bi-vocational role expect full-time support.

7. Acceptance. Encourage innovation and creativity in ministry so all sectors of society can be reached with the Gospel.

8. Fair Hearing. Provide a system of due process and interim compensation for pastors whom churches abuse. Pastors are too often cast aside at the will of a few malcontents and then viewed as suspect for the remainder of their ministry. Congregations who mistreat a pastor should be censored by the larger church body and held financially liable until the wronged pastor can be reassigned. On the contrary, a plan is also needed to be sure a pastor is faithful in doing ministry—no slothful servants should be tolerated in the Savior's service.

9. Spiritual Health. Promote the spiritual well-being of congregations rather than emphasizing numerical size alone. The work of all

God's called servants must be seen as valuable regardless of the size of church they serve.

10. Alongside Strength. Have all ecclesiastical leaders spend a minimum of two weeks each year in a local church with an average attendance of fewer than 100. Let them experience firsthand the pressures and possibilities pastors continually face. In such a one-on-one relationship, every pastor would get to see the heart of his leaders, and every official would feel the pulse of a local congregation.

X. The Right to Speak Out against Sin and Injustice

Pastors must be given the right to speak out on issues threatening the moral fiber of the nation, the church, and the family. There are times in every local church and every society, like Elijah's day, when someone must stand before the king to confront evil and speak forthrightly about the consequences of sin. Our world continues to decay morally at least in part because of the soft, timid words of the church concerning our local and national sins.

If pastors don't denounce sin, who will? Something must be done to stop the cancers of violence, immorality, brokenness, and greed. Pastors see the firsthand consequences of sin when it shows up in the lives of individuals and families. Ministers often face the gaping wounds resulting from alcohol, pornography, domestic violence, immorality, and selfishness. Yet little is said and less is done to heal them.

In this century, society has moved from puritanism to hedonism. An "anything goes" stance to outright silence in the church allows immorality to flourish. It's time to confront a depraved culture that kills the unborn, accepts perversions as alternative lifestyles, and tolerates violence at home and in the streets. It's time to speak. It's time to shout. It's time to yell "fire!"

Every pastor needs to be encouraged to speak a flaming word from God against national and individual sins in our culture. Let's take direction from the former Anglican Bishop of Southwark: "My diocese is said to be on the boil. If that is so, I accept it as a compliment. Boiling water is better than tepid. It can cleanse and generate power."[6]

God loathes sin in churches as much as He does in society. Thus, ministers must speak out against sin in their congregations, even though some churches have lower standards for members than the local Kiwanis Club. One church in Appalachia, in order to receive reduced postage, wrote on all its mail "non-prophet organization." But that's not the way God intends a church to be. Our Father wants His church pure and clean and exemplar so He can work through it without giving Himself a bad reputation. And He wants prophets to denounce sin.

Let one fact be clearly understood—God refuses to bless a church that accommodates wickedness in leadership on any level. Unfortunately, many churches have so watered down the message of righteousness that our Lord sees us as no better than the den of thieves He so angrily rebuked (John 2).

Every fair-minded person must encourage his pastor to speak the truth in love as a Christ-exalting corrective. The list of sins inside the church is long, frightening, and even nauseating: gossip, backbiting, slander, malice, immorality, spouse-swapping, financial scams, over-indulgence, and subtle worldliness in a thousand forms make the church too weak to fight and too guilty to seek God's face.

Many churches want only comforting words from their minister. But any congregation that keeps her pastor silent about sin will soon become as corrupt as the world. And any pastor who refuses to call people to repentance is guilty of malfeasance. Words of truth from Holy Scripture must be wholeheartedly supported. From the start of a minister's ministry in a new church setting, he must be given liberty to denounce sin and preach righteousness. Empower your pastor to speak redemptively against sin in society; encourage him to stand for righteousness; and support his efforts to expose darkness to the white light of God.

Let's Make a Difference

This chapter was not easy to write. It is filled with tender compassion and tough love for the church because we care. We want the church of Jesus Christ renewed in our time. The essential message we have written seems demanding and radical, and some readers may think, controversial. Some of what we have said leaves opportunity for misunderstanding or even objection. But try to hear our heart cry—too many pastors are forced to suffer for doing the right thing. Too many congregations are being sabotaged by shallow leaders who want control more than they want Christ and want power more than they want the Power.

Without spiritually committed, courageous pastors, the contemporary church will get steadily worse and society will become more corrupt. Pastors are not the only persons needed for this war, but it cannot be won without them. When pastors are in jeopardy, the church could lose the war. We are in a battle for the soul of the church and the eternal destiny of the lost. Winning will not be easy, but it is possible.

For too long the church has played into the enemy's hands by trashing pastors and by speaking too softly about what sin does in our lives, in families, and in society. We beg you to carefully consider what we have written. Weigh it conscientiously. Discuss it. Talk it over with your decision group. Ask your pastor to share his heart on these issues, perhaps for the first time. Pray about it. Then, do something to spiritually revolutionize the environment of your church.

It's time for lay pillars of the church to lock arms and join hearts with pastors. Let's move as one. Let's keep ourselves pure and holy so the Father will not be embarrassed to keep company with us. Let's ask the Author and Finisher of our faith to enable us. He will. Our Lord wants pastors and parishioners to move in a mighty, unified effort to change the world and revive the church.

Try in every feasible way to renew the spirit and stimulate your pastor's courage. Here's a short list on how to start.
- Love your pastor into greatness.
- Believe in him as a holy person.
- Apply her preaching to your life.
- Release him from repetitive routines.
- Make the logistics of her living as easy as possible.
- Don't waste his sacrifice.
- Encourage her to dream big dreams.
- Treat him as generously as you treat your boss.
- Start an affirmation campaign about your pastor today.

A Pastor's Bill of Rights

- Try to see your church through the eyes of the Savior.
- Commit to be a holy person who pleases God in all things.

RENEWAL STRATEGIES FOR CHURCH PILLARS
How to Liberate Your Pastor to Greatness

1. Encourage your pastor to dream.

2. Protect your pastor's privacy.

3. Promote adequate salary for your minister.

4. Encourage your pastor's professional development.

5. Champion your minister's need to have friends.

6. Shelter your pastor and family from ridiculous scrutiny.

7. Allow your leader the right to fail.

8. Provide your pastor the right of passage when needed.

9. Support your minister's right to organizational support.

10. Champion your leader's right to speak out against sin and injustice.

EPILOGUE
Is That a Cloud I See?

The church of Jesus Christ is ripe with growth all around the world. Every indication points to the fact that God is at work in an unusual way. It is estimated that 28,000 people a day accept the Savior in the People's Republic of China; 24,000 a day in Africa south of the Sahara Desert. More than 50,000 new churches are opened each year in South America. Yet in the United States, we close nearly eighty churches each week. Church growth is on the decline in a nation that has every advantage known to man. We wonder if we have taken seriously the call of God to build the church through evangelism and not gimmicks. As we travel the country, we see the church grasping for nearly anything that works, while in nation after nation the world is being saved one person at a time, by an army of laymen who still feel the salvation of mankind is their responsibility.

We are observers of the church. To be honest, we are not sure how the church will reach our lost nation if we fail to recognize sin as sin. Statistics say that in spite of all the seeker-sensitive methods used to reach the lost, fewer non-Christians are coming to church. Churches are not simply about filling seats; we are about preaching and teaching a message of repentance. Yet thousands of churches will not see one person come to know Christ this year. Why? Because they have lost a vision for the unsaved.

When asked, "What is the greatest challenge you face as a pastor?" ministers in our survey respond, "The apathy of laymen. Our people have very little passion for the message of the Great Commission." Well, folks, we had better generate some passion, or the world will continue to be unsaved and unimpressed by our "Madison Avenue" approach. Unbelievers are looking for something genuine, not just something that glitters. So what can we do?

PRAY for a revival in your own life. The prayer of David is a good place to begin. "Search me, O God, and know my heart; test me and know my anxious thoughts. See if there is any offensive way in me, and lead me in the way everlasting" (Ps. 139:23-24).

PRAY that God will burden your heart for the unsaved.

PRAY that God will place you in a field of spiritual harvest.

PRAY each day by name for the members of your family who are unsaved.

PRAY that your pastor and church leaders will have courage to preach and speak the Word of God with boldness.

PRAY that the spiritual leaders in your community will be bold enough to risk all for a genuine spiritual outpouring.

It's not too late. There is a cloud on the horizon. It's small, but it is filled with promise and looks like it might bring blessing and renewal to our land. The rain of God's blessing is on the horizon.

NOTES

Preface

1. Eugene H. Peterson, *The Message*, "1 Thessalonions 5: 12-13" (Colorado Springs: NavPress, 1993).

Chapter 1

1. *Monday Morning,* July 1995, 73.

2. H.B. London, Jr., Neil Wiseman, *Pastors at Risk* (Wheaton, Ill.: Victor Books, 1993), 34.

Chapter 2

1. Eugene H. Peterson, *The Message* (Colorado Springs: NavPress, 1993), 406–7.

2. William Barclay, *The Daily Study Bible: The Letters to the Philippians, Colossians, and Thessalonians* (Philadelphia: Westminster Press, 1957), 239.

3. ——, *The Daily Study Bible: The Letters to Timothy, Titus and Philemon* (Edinburgh: St. Andrews Press, 1956), 134.

4. Paul Barackman, *Proclaiming the New Testament: The Epistles to Timothy and Titus Commentary* (Grand Rapids: Baker, 1964), 65.

Chapter 3

1. Dr. Rodney Hunter, *Palm Beach Post,* October 20, 1995, 6D.

2. James Allen Sparks, *Pot-shots at the Preacher* (Nashville: Abingdon, 1977), 20.

3. Evan Esar, *20,000 Quips and Quotes* (New York: Barnes and Noble, 1968), 351.

4. Paul Meier, et al., *What They Didn't Teach You in Seminary* (Nashville: Nelson, 1993), 235.

5. Milo Arnold, *The Adventure of the Christian Ministry* (Kansas City: Beacon Hill, 1967), 14.

6. Daniel D. Walker, *Enemy in the Pew* (New York: Harper and Row, 1967), 82.

7. Robert Hudnut, *This People, This Parish* (Grand Rapids: Zondervan, 1986), 95.

8. John A. Sanford, *Ministry Burnout* (New York: Paulist Press, 1965), 26.

9. G. Lloyd Rediger, *Coping with Clergy Burnout* (Valley Forge, Pa.: Judson Press, 1982), 24.

10. Eugene H. Peterson, *Under the Unpredictable Plant* (Grand Rapids: Eerdmans, 1992), 5.

11. Jan G. Linn, *What Ministers Wish Church Members Knew* (St. Louis: Chalice Press, 1993), 71.

Chapter 4

1. Emmet Fox, *Making Your Life Worthwhile* (San Francisco: HarperSan Francisco, 1946), 211.

2. Jan G. Linn, *What Ministers Wish Church Members Knew* (St. Louis: Chalice Press, 1993), 11.

3. Louis E. Boone, *Quotable Business* (New York: Random House, 1992), 211.

4. "Essay Concerning Human Understanding" as quoted in *Concise Oxford Dictionary of Quotations* (Oxford: Oxford Press, 1994).

5. Louis E. Boone, *Quotable Business* , 85.

6. Evan Esar, *20,000 Quips and Quotes* (New York: Barnes and Noble, 1968), 589.

7. John Cowan, *The Common Table* (New York: HarperBusiness, 1993), 82–83.

8. James Bell, *Thoughts on Leadership* (Chicago: Triumph Books, 1995), 149.

9. Vance Havner, *Day by Day with Vance Havner* (Grand Rapids: Baker, 1953), 164.

10. Laurie Jones, *Jesus CEO* (New York: Hyperion Publishers, 1994), 109.

Chapter 5

1. Eugene H. Peterson, *The Message*, "John 3:17" (Colorado Springs: NavPress, 1993).

2. ———, *The Message*, 410

Chapter 6

1. Janis Allen, as quoted by Bob Nelson in *1001 Ways to Reward Employees* (New York: Workman Publishing, 1994), 30.

Chapter 7

1. Eugene H. Peterson, *The Message* (Colorado Springs: NavPress, 1993).

2. Lloyd J. Ogilvie, *The Commentator's Commentary*, Vol. 5 (Waco, Texas: Word, 1983), 75.

3. Dom Helder Camara, *A Thousand Reasons for Living* (Philadelphia: Fortress Press, 1981), 85.

4. Peterson, *The Message*, "James 3:6-10,"

5. Ibid.

6. James Allen Sparks, *Pot-shots at the Preacher* (Nashville, Abingdon, 1977), 97.

Chapter 8

1. Vance Havner, *In Tune with Heaven* (Grand Rapids: Baker, 1990), 57.

2. Charles Colson, *The Body* (Dallas: Word, 1992), 187.

3. Malcolm Muggeridge, *Confessions of a Twentieth-Century Pilgrim* (San Francisco: Harper & Row, 1988), 139.

4. Richard Halverson, *The Living Body* (Gresham, Ore.: Vision House, 1994), 48.

Chapter 9

1. Louis E. Boone, *Quotable Business* (New York: Random House, 1992), 200.

2. *Bathroom Book*, Vol. 1 (Salt Lake City: Compact Classics, 1992), 3-B4.

3. James B. Simpson, *Simpson's Contemporary Quotes* (New York: Houghton Mifflin, 1988), 65.

4. Ibid., 239.

5. From an address given at the Sorbonne, April 23, 1910.

6. Robert K. Hudnut, *Surprised by God* (New York: Association Press, 1967), 68.